S0-AEJ-496

Fifteenth Century English Prayers and Meditations

Garland Reference Library of the Humanities (Vol. 19)

Fifteenth Century English Prayers and Meditations

A Descriptive List of Manuscripts in the British Library

compiled by
Peter Revell

Garland Publishing, Inc., New York & London

1975

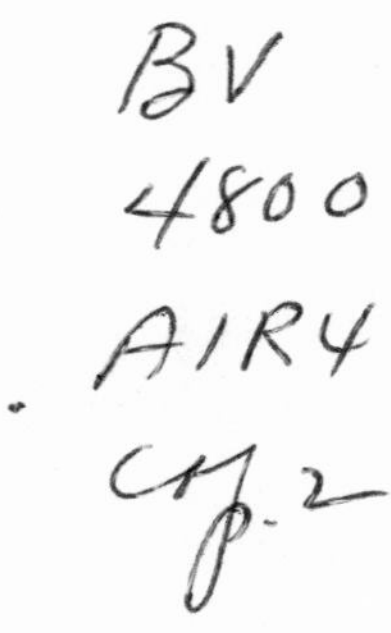

Library of Congress Cataloging in Publication Data

Revell, Peter.
Fifteenth-century English prayers and meditations.

(Garland reference library of the humanities ; v. 19)
Includes indexes.
1. Devotional literature--Manuscripts--Catalogs.
I. British Library. II. Title.
Z6611.T3R48 [BV4801] 016.242 75-6579
ISBN 0-8240-1098-1

Printed in the United States of America

CONTENTS

PRAYERS

PREFACE

This descriptive list is intended to have two main areas of interest — in church history, as a survey of some of the relevant background material for research into the spiritual life of fifteenth century England, and in the study of Middle English literature as a guide to a number of minor and often overlooked texts. The disposition of the items is intended to serve the first area of interest and the indices the second. The list attempts to cover only items included in the chief British collection of manuscripts, but reference is made in the notes to additional copies of texts in the other major national collections.

A meditation is defined by the Oxford Dictionary as 'That kind of private devotional exercise which consists in the continuous application of the mind to the contemplation of some religious truth, mystery or object of reverence, in order that the soul may increase in love of God and holiness of life.' This definition has been used, as far as my limited judgement allowed, in deciding which texts qualify for inclusion as meditations. The definition has been so interpreted as to exclude tracts and poems which are merely expository or hortatory in tone (for example, tracts on the Seven Deadly Sins, expositions and moral treatises on the Ten Commandments, the Creed, etc.), or which are primarily paraphrases of Scriptural texts. Works of this nature are chiefly concerned with the inculcation of the formal elements of Christian doctrine and their application in daily life, whereas the distinguishing quality of the meditation is that it approaches the *locutio ad Deum* characteristic of prayer. The close connection between meditation and prayer has been emphasised by Professor David Knowles: 'The soul at her entrance upon a spiritual course ordinarily begins by making use of vocal prayer and meditation upon the truths of religion, together with certain practices of mortification and a regular life.' (*The English Mystics*, p.34).

Inevitably, many items were difficult to classify and the choice was on occasions necessarily arbitrary. In particular, questions of form called for special consideration of the following categories:

(a) works in dialogue form,

(b) works on moral subjects in which the treatment was essentially that of the meditation,

(c) narrative works containing matter of the type found in religious meditations.

It was finally decided to admit the first two categories and exclude the third. The question whether a lyric on a religious topic might truly be classified as a meditation or prayer also presented certain difficulties, since the internal raising of the mind in the contemplation of religious truths and mysteries may here be a part of the literary technique of the writer rather than his spiritual intent. Lyrics which in subject matter and general tone are similar in character to prose meditations have, however, been included.

Only works originally composed in the fifteenth century or by an author whose life falls largely in the fifteenth century have been included as items in the list. Later copies are noted among the other copies but not as distinct items. The dates quoted are those given in the British Museum (now British Library) catalogues, supplemented by additional data supplied in printed editions of certain texts. The date of manuscripts (which is, of course, not necessarily the date of original composition) is given in the form 's.xv.in' for first half of the fifteenth century, 's.xv.ex' for second half of the fifteenth century, 's.xv.med.' for mid-fifteenth century, or simply 's.xv.' when the manuscript cannot be dated more closely than this. Fifteenth century copies of earlier texts have been (it is hoped, entirely) eliminated by reference to Wells's *Manual of Writings in Middle English;* Brown and Robbins, *Index of Middle English verse,* with Supplement by Robbins and Cutler; the Bodley *Catalogue of Western Manuscripts*; M.R. James's catalogues of manuscripts in the libraries of Cambridge; and printed editions of texts by Rolle and others. One sixteenth century manuscript, Arundel 285, has been included, since it supplied references to a body of fifteenth century prayers not represented elsewhere in the British Library's collection. As a rule, fifteenth century reworkings of earlier material (for example, some texts of the Charters of Christ and some of the lyrics) have been included. In the transcription, the various methods of abbreviating the name 'Jesu', e.g. Ihc, Jhu, ihu, and so on, have been expanded into the one form 'Jh*es*u'.

My indebtedness to the published catalogues of the collections of the British Library, Department of Manuscripts will be obvious throughout this list. For details of Additional Manuscripts and Egerton Manuscripts acquired since those included in the published catalogues I have been dependent on the unpublished Hand-Lists of Recent Accessions available in the Manuscript Students' Room. The Additional Manuscripts have been checked to Add.MS 58,234 and the Egerton Manuscripts to Egerton MS 3,795, covering accessions to the collections as far as the middle of 1973.

It is a pleasant duty to record my thanks for help of various kinds in the preparation of this list. For advice and helpful suggestions at an early stage in its preparation I am grateful to the late Professor Francis Wormald, to Mr. Julian Roberts, and most especially to Mr. Andrew G. Watson. For help in bringing the list to publication I wish to thank Mr. Peter Kemeny, and also the authorities of the University of London Library. Much of my work has been in the British Library; I am glad to have this opportunity to thank the staff of the Manuscript Students' Room for many kindnesses.

P.R.

SELECT BIBLIOGRAPHY

CATALOGUES

A comprehensive list of the catalogues of the British Library, Department of Manuscripts which are in regular use may be found in *The Catalogues of the Manuscript Collections in the British Museum,* by T.C. Skeat (Published by the Trustees of the British Museum, 1962). The following are the chief items consulted in the preparation of the present work.

British Museum. *Index to the Sloane Manuscripts in the British Museum*, by Edward J.L. Scott. London, 1904.

_____________. *Index to the Additional Manuscripts...preserved in the British Museum and acquired in the years 1783-1835.* London, 1849.

_____________. *List of Additions to the Manuscripts in the British Museum in the years 1836-1840.* London, 1843, and subsequent volumes covering Additional Manuscripts acquired to 1945. These volumes also include descriptions of the Egerton Manuscripts and additions to the Egerton collection.

_____________. *Catalogue of Manuscripts in the British Museum.* Vol.I, Part I. The Arundel Manuscripts. London, 1834, and index vol., 1840.

_____________. *A Catalogue of the Manuscripts in the Cottonian Library deposited in the British Museum.* London, 1802.

Smith, Thomas. *Catalogus Librorum Manuscriptorum Bibliothecae Cottonianae.* Oxford, 1696.

British Museum. *A Catalogue of the Harleian Manuscripts in the British Museum.* 4 vols. London, 1808-12.

_____________. *A Catalogue of the Lansdowne Manuscripts in the British Museum.* London, 1819.

______________. *Catalogue of Western Manuscripts in the Old Royal and King's Collections.* 4 vols. London, 1921.

Bodleian Library. *Summary Catalogue of Western Manuscripts.* 8 vols. Oxford, 1895-1953.

Cambridge University Library. *A Catalogue of the Manuscripts preserved in the Library of the University of Cambridge.* 6 vols. Cambridge, 1856-67.

James, M.R. Catalogues of manuscripts in the libraries of Cambridge colleges. 1895-1925.

Bateson, Mary, ed. *Catalogue of the Library of Syon Monastery.* Cambridge, 1898.

EDITIONS OF TEXTS. Listed by editor.

Allen, H.E. *Writings ascribed to Richard Rolle.* London, 1927.

______________. *Richard Rolle, English Writings.* Oxford, 1931.

Bazire, Joyce. *The Metrical Life of St. Robert of Knaresborough.* (Early English Text Society, Original Series, no.228.) London, 1953.

Brown, Carleton. *Religious Lyrics of the XVth Century.* Oxford, 1939.

Comper, Frances M.M. *Spiritual Songs from English MSS of the Fourteenth to Sixteenth Centuries.* London, 1936.

Cumming, W.P. *The Revelations of Saint Birgitta.* (E.E.T.S., O.S.178.) London, 1929.

Day, M. *The Wheatley Manuscript.* (E.E.T.S., O.S.155.) London, 1921.

Furnivall, F.J. *Hymns to the Virgin and Christ...and other religious poems.* (E.E.T.S., O.S.24.) London, 1867.

______________. *Political, Religious and Love Poems from Lambeth MS.306 and other sources.* (E.E.T.S., O.S.15.) London, 1866.

Halliwell, J.O. *A Selection from the Minor Poems of Dan John Lydgate.* (Percy Society, Vol.2) London, 1840.

Horstmann, C. *The Minor Poems of the Vernon Manuscript.* Vol.I; Vol.II ed. by F.J. Furnivall. (E.E.T.S., O.S.98 & 117.) London, 1892-1901.

______________. *Yorkshire Writers: Richard Rolle of Hampole, an English Father of the Church and his followers.* 2 vols. London, 1895-6.

Hudleston, Roger. *Revelations of Divine Love shewed to a devout ankress by name Julian of Norwich.* 2nd ed. London, 1952. (1st pubd., 1927.)

MacCracken, H.N. *The Minor Poems of John Lydgate.* Vol.I. Religious Poems. (E.E.T.S., Extra Series, no.107.) London, 1911.

Morris, Richard. *Legends of the Holy Rood, Symbols of the Passion and Cross-Poems.* (E.E.T.S., O.S.46) London, 1871.

Reynolds, Anna Maria. *Julian of Norwich; the shorter version of sixteen revelations of divine love.* London, 1958.

Sandys, William. *Christmas Carols.* London, 1833.

Walsh, James. *The Revelations of Divine Love of Julian of Norwich.* London, 1961.

OTHER SOURCES

Bale, John. *Index of British and Other Writers,* ed. R.L. Poole. Oxford, 1902.

Brown, Carleton and Rossell Hope Robbins. *The Index of Middle English Verse.* New York, 1943.

______________. *Supplement to the Index of Middle English Verse,* by Rossell Hope Robbins and John L. Cutler. Lexington, 1965.

Butterworth, C.C. *The English Primers, 1529-1545.* Philadelphia, 1953.

Crehan, J.H. *Father Thurston : a memoir with a bibliography of his writings.* London, 1953.

Knowles, David. *The English Mystics.* London, 1927.

______________. *The English Mystical Tradition.* London, 1961.

Lubbock, S.G. *A Memoir of M.R. James, with a list of his writings by A.F. Schofield.* Cambridge, 1939.

Maskell, William. *Monumenta Ritualia Ecclesiae Anglicanae.* Vol.3. Oxford, 1882.

Spalding, M.C. *The Middle English Charters of Christ.* Bryn Mawr, 1914.

Tanner, Thomas. *Bibliotheca Britannico-Hibernica.* London, 1748.

Thurston, H. *Familiar Prayers, their origin and history.* London, 1953.

Vacant, A. and E. Mangenot. *Dictionnaire de Theologie Catholique.* 15 vols. Paris, 1909-50. (cf. Vol.13, article on 'Prière'.)

Wells, John Edwin. *Manual of the Writings in Middle English, 1050-1400.* London, 1916, and Supplements.

Wilmart, André. *Auteurs Spitituels et Textes Devots du moyen age latin.* Paris, 1932.

MEDITATIONS

I. THE TRINITY AND GOD THE FATHER

1. On the Trinity. Royal 18 A X.f.15. s.xv.in.
30 lines to page.

Beg. SEynt Johan seyth in his gospel that ther ben thre persones in the trinite

Ends f.15b. as we desire to be rewardit in heuene aboue.

2. Poem on a vision of the Blessed Trinity - 'Benedicta sit sancta Trinitas'.
Harl.2255.f.150b. s.xv.
9 stanzas of 8 lines.

Beg. UNdir a park ful prudently pyght
A perillous path men passyd by

Ends f.151b. Disposing our deth daily be dignite.

Pr. by Carleton Brown, Religious Lyrics of the XVth Century, pp.69-71, from this MS.

3. A good question to God. Royal 18 A X.f.10. s.xv.in.
30 lines to page.

Beg. A sely soule askid of god oure stedefast lord clennes of soule

Ends f.10b. nat after thyn felyng but after myn dome.

4. Poem -'Misericordias Domini in eternum cantabo' - Lydgate.

Harl.2255.f.17. s.xv.
24 stanzas of 8 lines.

R. Misericordias domini in eternum cantabo.

Beg. Alle goostly songis & ympnes that be songe
Of Oold and newe remembrid in scripture

Ends f.21. Eternally thy mercyes they do syng.

Col. Explicit quod lidgate.

Other copies, Jesus Camb.56,f.41a; Trinity Camb. 601,f.193b. Pr. by MacCracken, E.E.T.S., E.S.cvii, pp.71-7 from this MS.

5. Poem - 'Benedictus Deus in donis suis' - Lydgate.

Harl.2255.f.142. s.xv.
9 stanzas of 8 lines.

R. Benedictus deus in donis suis.

Beg. GOd departith his gyfftys dyversly
To summe he yevith witt & discrecioun

Ends f.143. Seyth what god sent blessyd mut he be.

Col. Explicit quod lydgate.

Another copy, Bodl.798,f.31b. Pr. by MacCracken, E.E.T.S., E.S.cvii, pp.7-9 from the Bodley MS.

6. Devout meditation on the goodness of God.

Add.10,596.f.49. s.xv.
22 lines to page.

R. Here bigynneþ a deuout meditacioun a man to þenke wiþinne him on þe godenes of oure blessid lord at mornn or at euen as he is disposid & haþ leiser.

Beg. Blessid lord þat madist al þing of nouȝt kepist & gouernist alle creaturis in heuene & in erþe, worschip laude & praising be to þee

Ends f.54. þi merci and goodnes þat hath noon eende Amen.

7. Poem on God's help - Lydgate. Harl.2255.f.148. s.xv.
13 stanzas of 8 lines.

Beg. GOd is myn helpere and ay shal be
My cheef protectour and diffence

Ends f.150. Wheer god lyst helpe ther is no drede.

Col. Explicit quod lydgate.

Pr. by MacCracken, E.E.T.S., E.S.cvii, pp.27-30, from this MS.

8. Of God's justice. Add.37,049.f.96. s.xv.in.
52 lines to page.

Beg. Mykil folkes þer is þat hopes þat god wil dampne no man

Ends f.96b. Bottom of leaf damaged. Imperf.

With drawings.

9. A devout treatise concerning the love of God.
Harl.1706.f.154b. s.xv.
22 lines to page, double-columned.

List of contents ff.154b-155b.

Text beg. f.155b. IN þe bygynnynge and endynge
of alle good werkes worschyppe
and þanckynge

Ends f.204b. haue wrytten vn to þe þese fewe wordys
in helpe of þi soule Deo gracias.

II. CHRIST

10. Mirror of the Life of Christ - Bonaventura.

Add.30,031.f.1. s.xv in.

R. HEre bigynneþ þe prohemie of þe book þat is clepid þe mirour of þe blessid lif of Jhesu cryst

Beg. These ben þe wordis of þe grete doctour & holy apostil paul consyderynge þat þe gostly lyuynge of alle trewe cristene creatures

Ends f.101b. And blessid be þe name of oure lord Jhesu in his modor marie now & euere w^{t}outen ende Amen.

Col. Explicit speculum vite cristi.

Concluding section:

f.101b.R. A short tretys of þe hiȝest & most worþi sacrament of cristes blesside body and þe meruayles þerof.

Beg. MEmoriam fecit mirabilium suorum misericors & miserator deus estam dedit timentibus se. Þese wordes of david in þe sauter seid in prophecie

Ends f.110. by vertue & grace of þy life blessid w^{t}oute endynge Amen

Col. Explicit speculum vite cristi complete. Iste liber translatum fuit de latino in anglicum per dominum Richardum loue Priorem monasterij de mounte grace ordinis cartusiensis.

Ff.110b-111b contains a list of contents, dividing the work into 64 chapters.

Translation of the Meditationes Vitae Christi, attributed to St. Bonaventura. Peltier(Bonaventurae Opera, xii, p.xlii) states that the work is not by Bonaventura but by a Franciscan of San Gimignano in Tuscany or the neighbourhood, perhaps Johannes de

Caulibus. Possibly translated by Nicholas Love, prior of Mount Grace, early in 15th century. Warton (Hist. of English Poetry, ed. 1840, ii, p.320) ascribes the translation to John Morton, an Augustinian. For a translation into French, cf. Royal 20 B.IV. Caxton pr. the Myrrour of the Blessed Lyf of Jesu Crist in 1488; de Worde in 1525. Cf. also C. Fischer, Die Meditationes Vitae Christi. Ihre handschriftliche Ueberlieferung und die Verfasserfräge. (Archivum Franciscanum Historicum, xxv, 1932).

11. Another copy, Add.19,901.f.l. s.xv.in.

Divided into 56 chapters, with the treatise on the Sacrament.

12. Another copy, Add.21,006,f.l. s.xv.in.

Divided into 50 chapters, ends imperf.

13. Another copy, Add.11,748.ff.140-144. s.xv.

A single chapter.

14. Another copy, Arundel 112.f.l. s.xv.

Divided into 66 chapters, with the treatise on the Sacrament.

15. Another copy, Arundel 364.f.l. s.xv.

Divided into 44 chapters, with the treatise on the Sacrament.

16. Another copy, Add.11,565.f.l. s.xv.

Imperf. at beginning.

17. Another copy, Royal 18 C X.f.1. s.xv.med.

Imperf. at end.

18 Egerton 2,658.f.1. s.xv.

Extract or abridgement of the section on the Passion, Resurrection and Ascension.

19. Add.36,983.f.118. s.xiv.ex.

Verse translation, beg. 'Allmyghty God in trenite', of part of the pseudo-Bonaventurian 'Life of Christ'. Considerably earlier in date than the prose version.

20. Life of Christ - Ludolphus of Saxony. Add.16,609.f.2. s.xv.ex.

R. Here foloweth the prologe of ffrere Gwylliam lemenaud of thordre of the ffrers mynors of fraunce translatoure of this noble & proufitable booke called the lyve of cryste oute of laten into ffrenche which nowe is translated oute of french toung into ower tounge of Englissh.

Beg. JEsus the sonne of godde and second persone in the trinite by whome the fader hathe created

Ends f.236b. and he not reputede for a foole and a mad man.

Translated into English from the French version of Friar Guillaume le Menaud, made from the original Latin of Ludolphus of Saxony.

Charters of Christ

M.C. Spalding, The Middle English Charters of Christ, (Bryn Mawr, 1914) distinguishes two forms, which she calls the Short Charter and the Long Charter. The former originated in the 14th century, as did the shortest form (Version A) of the Long Charter. Two versions of the Long Charter (Versions B and C) are, however, substantially 15th century compositions and are noted here. Cf. Spalding, op.cit., p.lxviiff. for a discussion of the relationships of the different versions.

i. Version B.

21. Cotton. Caligula. A.II.f.77a. s.xv
In couplets, 416 lines.

R. Carta Jhesu Cristi

Beg. Who so wyll ouer-rede thys boke
And with hys gostlye ye þer-on loke

Ends Graunte vs to se þy holy face Amen

Col. Explicit.

Pr. by Spalding, pp.47-81.

22. Harley 2382.f.111b. s.xv.

Another copy. 414 lines, omitting last couplet of Cotton Caligula A II text.

Ends f.117b. that of myght made al thyng.

Col. Explicit
Testamentum Cristi.

Other copies, Camb. Univ. Ff.2.38,f.39b; Camb. Univ. Ii.4.9,f.42b; Camb. Univ. Ee.2,15,f.90a; Camb. Univ. Ii.3.26.f.235a.

ii. Version C.

23. Royal 17 C.XVII.f.112b. s.xv in.
618 lines.

Beg. He þat wyll rede ouer þis boke
& with hys gostly high þer-in loke

Ends f.116b. þat of noght made alle thyng.

Pr. by Horstmann, Minor Poems of the Vernon MS., pp.637-657.

24. Poem to Christ - 'Criste qui lux es et dies' - Lydgate.
Harl.2251.f.235b. s.xv.
7 stanzas of 8 lines.

Beg. Christ that art both day and light
And sothfast sonne of al gladnesse

Ends f.236. ffor whiche we synge In Joye and woo
Deo patri sit gloria.

Another copy, Trinity Camb. 600, p.195.

Pr. by MacCracken, E.E.T.S. E.S.cvii, pp.235-7, from the Trinity Camb. MS.

25. Prayer - 'Christe qui lux es et dies'.
Harl.665.f.299b. s.xv.
7 stanzas of 4 lines.

R. Jhesu nostra redemptor.

Beg. Criste qui lux es (&c.)
Cryst þat art boþe ly3t & day
Derkenesse of ny3t þou doyst a way

Ends f.300. I flarysched the eeres feedyt.

Cf. Carleton Brown, Register of Middle English Verse, II, p.81 and Zupitza, Archiv. lxxxv, pp.45-6.

26. Poem - Panem Vitae. Harl.3810 (Part 1).f.10b. s.xv.
24 lines to page.

Beg. Cryst þat was crowned with caytyfes vnkynd
Graunt me graþli to kenne this

Ends f.13. Þat leveþ in god in forme of brede.

Col. Explicit panem vite.

Other copies, Camb. Univ. Ee.4.35,f.3a; Ff.2.38,f.54a; Ff.5.48,f.116b (variant text). Pr. by C.H. Hartshorne, Ancient Metrical Tales, London 1829 from the Camb. MS. Ff.2.38 and by Jordan, Englische Studien, XLI, pp.256-61 from this MS.

27. Meditations on the Life and Passion of Christ. Add.11,307.f.7a. s.xv.in.
2,252 lines in couplets.

Beg. Heyl be þou, sone of þe fader aboue,
Þat man bycome for mannes loue
Ends f.87b. Godes sone wiþouten gynnyng. Amen.

Pr. by C. d'Evelyn (E.E.T.S. O.S.158, 1921), who dates the original composition in the second half of 14th century. This is the only MS. The work is based on John of Hoveden's Meditacio.

28. Poem on Christ. Add.37,049.f.25. s.xv.in.
45 lines.

Beg.f.25. If þai do so, he wil þaim safe.
As walnot barke his hare is ȝalowe
In summer ceson when it is grene

Ends f.25. Wher þ^{u} art emprowre kyng & lorde. Amen.

Cat. - "last 45 lines of a poem describing the appearance of Christ(?)," with a drawing (Arbor Amoris).

29. Poem on the words of Christ to the Blessed Virgin. - Lydgate.
Harl.2251.f.78. s.xv.
3 stanzas of 7 lines.

Beg. My fader above, beholdynge thy mekenesse
As dewe on Rosis doth his bawme sprede

Ends f.78. Whan they me pray for helpe in thy presence.

Pr. by MacCracken, E.E.T.S. E.S.cvii,p.235, from this MS.

30. Poem to Christ - 'Do mercy to fore þi judgement'. Harl.1704.f.26b. s.xv.
82 lines.

Beg. There is no creature but one
Maker of alle creatures

Ends f.27b. Betwyxe vs and thy Jugement. Amen.

Another copy, Lambeth 853, p.54. Pr. by Day, E.E.T.S., O.S.155, pp.65-7 from Add.39,574,f.51a; Furnivall, E.E.T.S., O.S.24, pp.18-21 from the Lambeth MS.; Brunner, Archiv CXXXII, pp.321-3 from Add.31042; Patterson, The Middle English Penitential Lyric, pp.85-8 from this MS.

31. Another copy. Add.31,042.f.123a.

32. Another copy. Add.39,574.f.51a.

33. Poems on the washing of Christ's feet by Mary Magdalen. Royal 17C.XVII.f.103b. s.xv.in.
37 lines to page.
87 couplets.

1. Forthe come on of þe pharaseus
A grete lorde halden emang þe iewes

Ends f.103b. To þe syns I am reles.
61 couplets

2. Beg.f.103b. On maners [sic] penance to halde
Man in þis warld trought god es kalde.

Ends f.106. Þe warkys of mercy to dyspyce.

34. Treatise on the Passion. Arund.286.f.1. s.xv.
29 lines to page.

F.1. 1.1. [Red] one line indecipherable.
1.2. A worschipful lady hauynge a symple spirit ful of heuenly desires

Ends f.19b. þis grace vs graunte þat wiþ his blood vs bou3t Crist Jhesu goddes sone Amen.

35. The passioun of Christ. Arund.285.f.159b. s.xvi.
8 stanzas of 8 lines.

R. The passioun of Christ.

Beg. Compatience persis reuth & marcy stoundis
In myddis my hert and thirlis throw þe vanis.

Ends f.161. Sen þat þi passioun purgit my trespas.

Col. Explicit.

Pr. by Carleton Brown, Religious Lyrics of the XVth Century, pp.131-3.

36. Notes on the Passion, etc. Add.33,381. s.xv.
29 lines in all.

Beg.f.151b. Crist as þu leffyste withouten in word

Ends f.151b. Final lines illegible.

37. Meditations on the Passion. Arund.285.f.125b. s.xvi.

A series of meditations, of 3-6 lines each, arranged for each day of the week under 8 or more numbered articles and with special meditations 'Befor þe meit' and 'Efter þe meit', and 'Befor þe supper', and 'Efter þe supper'. Each numbered meditation begins 'O lord Jhesu, þat þollit ...' or 'O Lord Jhesu þat offerand þi passioun' or a variation on this pattern. The prayers 'after meit' are some 30 lines long.

The meditations for Saturday have the numbered articles omitted; the prayers before and after 'meit' and 'supper' are followed by 'þe houris of oure ladyis dollouris'.

The meditations for Sunday are only those before and after 'meit' and 'supper'.

Beg. FOR MONUNday þe first artikill think
how Jhesus witand quhat pain he was to
suffer was sad and dolorus

Ends f.144 with 'Passand to sleip ane orisoun'
6 lines beginning 'Think þat þe rest of
hevin amang angellis and all sanctis'

With an insert woodcut of Christ crucified.

38. The Passioun of Crist - Walter Kennedy.
Arund.285.f.5b. s.xvi.

f.5b. coloured woodcut of the Scourging inserted.
In red, rubric below 'Heir begynnis þe
proloug of þe passioun of Crist compilit
be Mr Walter Kennedy'.

Beg. HAIL CRIstin kny3t haill etern confortour
Haill Riall king in trone celistiall

10 stanzas of 8 and 7 lines.

Ends f.7b. Sa in yis hope my purpous woll I found
Explicit prologus Incipit Passio.

f.8. GOD OF of [sic] his grace and gudnes
infinit
Sa nobill maid þe man his creatour

243 stanzas of 8 and 7 lines.

Ends f.46b. In hevin empire þat þou þi face may se
Without end Amen for þi marcy.

Col. Heir endis the passioun of our Lord Jhesu
Crist compilit be Maister Walter Kennedy.

Rubrics in red divide the poem into sections,
e.g. 'At cumplin tyme', 'At euensang', 'The
fourt apperacioun to Sanct Peter', 'Ferria
quinta ad vesperas', etc.

Pr. by Schipper, Poems of Walter Kennedy,
pp.25-94.

39. On the Passion of our Lord.
Harl.1706.f.210. s.xv.
24 stanzas,
mostly of 4 lines.

R. As clerkes seyne and specyally seynt Anselme þere were vppon þe blessed and most gloryouse body of oure lorde Jhesu cryste open woundes by nombre v.þousand iiij hundred seuenty and fyue. howe oure lorde Jhesu seuene tymes bleed for vs.

Beg. Jhesu þat alle þis worlde haste wrouȝte
And of a cleene virgyn so tokeste oure kynde

Ends f.212. We maye reioyce euer þi presence.

Pr. by Carleton Brown, Religious Lyrics of the XVth Century, pp.133-5 from a Huntington Library MS.

40. Meditation on the Passion. Add.37,049.f.68b.
s.xv.in.
64 lines.

R. Here begynnes a deuowte meditacion of þe passione of Jhesus criste after þe seuen howres of þe day ordand in holy kirke how a man sal remembyr þaim.

Beg. f.68b. Man take hede on þe day or on þe nyght
How Criste was taken with grete myght

Ends f.68b. if þu blis wil gett þu put it euer to godenes
Euer more in al distres.

16 couplets on the Hours of the Passion, with a parallel series of 16 couplets on the five senses; with drawings.

41. Devout complaint of the passion of our Lord - Lydgate. Harl.7333.f.147. s.xv.

51 lines to page, double-columned.

R. Here nowe folowithe and begynnethe a devoute compleynte Off the passioune of oure lorde Jhesus criste mede by Lidgate with þe Refrayde [sic] man þenke on my passioune.

Beg. MAn to Reforme þyne exile and þi leste ffrome paradys place of moste plesaunce

Ends f.147b. þan ofte thenkynge ouer Cristes passioun.

Other copies, Bodl. 798,f.12a; Camb. Un. Kk.1.6.f.194a; Trinity Camb. 601,f.189b. Pr. by MacCracken, E.E.T.S., E.S.cvii, pp.216-21, from the Bodley MS.

42. Another copy, Harley 372,f.54.

43. Another copy, Add.31,042.f.94b.

44. Dolorous complaint of Our Lord upon the Cross. Arund.285.f.164b. s.xvi.

23 stanzas of 6 lines.

R. The Dollorus complant of oure lorde Apoune þe croce crucifyit.

Beg. Now herkynnis wordis wunder gude
How Jhesus crist hang on þe rude

Ends f.168. In hevin but end Amen.

45. Another copy, Add.37,049.f.45b.

Beg. ȝit stand a while & þink no lange

46. Another copy, Add.37,049.f.676.

Beg. Herkyn wordes swete and goode

Nos.45-6 together represent the complete poem, as No.44.

47. Dialogue on the Passion.
Royal 18 A X.f.126b. s.xv.in.
41 stanzas of 13 lines, but stanzas 2 and 41 irregular.

Beg. O litel whyle lesteneþ to me
Ententyfly, so haue ȝe blys

Ends f.130b. Graunte vs þe lyfe of grace. Amen.

Pr. from this MS. by Morris, Legends of the Holy Rood, (E.E.T.S. 1871, pp.197-209).

48. Verses on the Symbols of the Passion. Royal 17 A XXVII.f.72b. s.xv.in.
c.20 lines to page.

Beg. O vernacule I honoure him & the
Þat þe made þorow his preuite

Ends f.80. for mari loue þi moder fre amen

Following this An epilogue of 32 lines, concerning indulgences,

Beg. Þese armus of crist boþ god & man
sent petur þe pop discriuet hem

Ends Of pardon þus popus haþ graunted þe.

Accompanied by crude illustrations of the emblems of the Passion, etc.

Other copies: Bodl. 2975; Bodl. 21575,f.56a; Bodl. 29110; Queen's Oxf. 207.f.165b; Camb. Univ. Ii.6.43,f.103a, etc. Cf. Robbins, MLR XXXIV, pp.415-21.

49. Another copy, Add.11,748,f.140b.

Beg. veronicle y honoure hym in the

70 lines, in couplets.

50. Another copy, Add.22,029.

Beg. The vernacul I honowre hym [in the]

Vellum roll. Pr. by Morris, Legends of the Holy Rood, (E.E.T.S., O.S.46), pp.170-196, from this MS.

51. Another copy, Add.32,006.

Beg. O [remainder illegible].

Longer version, with 34 line suffix on indulgences. 240 lines in all, in couplets. Vellum roll.

52. Poem on the Crucifixion.
Add.37,049.f.45. s.xv.in.
58 lines.

Beg. f.45. Thy myghty mercy kyng of blis
My syn & me be þu ay betwyx

Ends f.45. To his honour lofyng & complacense
Amen.

With drawing of the Crucifixion. Pr. by Comper, Spiritual Songs, pp.131-2, from this MS.

53. Poem on the Five Wounds - (dialogue between the soul and the body).
Add.37,049.f.20. s.xv.
36 lines in all.

R. Beati mundo corde qui ip[si Deum] vident. [partly trimmed away].

Begins f.20. Querela anima
O man vnkynde
hafe in mynde
My paynes smert

Ends f.20. Þat we may alle
In to þi halle
With ioy cum sone
Amen.

Accompanied by drawing of the crucified Christ, a figure kneeling at foot and a representation of the Sacred Heart. Pr. by Carleton Brown, Religious Lyrics of the XVth Century, pp.168-9.

54. Four poems on the Five Wounds.
Add.37,049.f.24. s.xv.

1. Not the same as poem on f.20 of this MS.
6 lines.

Beg. O man kynde
hafe in þi mynde
my passion smert

Ends lo here my hert.

Another copy, Bodl. 819,f.14b.

2. Triplet, viz. 3 lines.

Þe nowmer of Jhesu cristes wowndes
Ar fyve þowsande foure hondreth sexty & fyftene
Þe whilk his body war felt & sene.

Other copies, Bodl. 10234,f.10b; Bodl. 21573, f.70b; Trinity Camb. 601,f.278b. Pr. in Early English Carols, p.401.

3. Beg. Jhesu my lyf my ioy my reste 6 lines
Þi perfite luf close in my breste

Ends Þat I may reyne in ioy euermore with þe.

Pr. by Carleton Brown, Religious Lyrics of the XVth Century, p.102.

4. Beg. The nowmer of our lords droppes alle
I wil reherse in seuerall

Ends Þis is þe nowmer of þaim alle.

55. Poem - 'Quinque vulnera' - Lydgate.
Cotton. Caligula.A.II.f.134b. s.xv.med.
5 stanzas of 8 lines.

R. Quinque vulnera.

Beg. Vppon the crosse y nayled was for the
Suffred deth to pay þy raunsoun

Ends f.134b. At her request be to vs merciable Amen.

Col. Explicit.

Other copies, Bodl. 798,f.14b; Bodl. 1475,f.50a; Bodl. 4119,f.4a (st.5 only); Bodl. 14526,f.31b; St. John's Oxf.56,f.84a; Camb. Univ. Hh.4.12.f.85a; Camb. Univ. Kk.1.6.f.196b; Jesus Camb. 56,f.70b. etc. Pr. by MacCracken, E.E.T.S., E.S.cvii, pp.252-4, from Bodl. 798, and elsewhere; cf. Fehr, Archiv. CVI, pp.63-4.

56. Another copy, Harley 2255,f.111.

57. Another copy, Harley 5396,f.294.

58. Another copy, Add.5465,f.68b.

59. Another copy, Add.29,729,f.131 (4 stanzas only).

60. Poem on the Resurrection.
Lansdowne 388.f.373. s.xv.
c.33 lines to page.

Beg. Alle myghty lorde in Trenyte
o god an persones thre

Ends f.380b. My leue frendis þat þis boke herde
graunte me þis [catch-phrase]

Imperf. at end. Apparently based on the Southern Resurrection, cf. Brown and Robbins, Index of ME Verse, item 1546.

61. Poem on the Resurrection.
Royal 17 C.XVII.f.152b. s.xv.in.
40 lines to page, double-columned.

Beg. [H]er begynnes a new lesson
Off crystys ressurrecion

Ends f.155b. Wyt hym to won withoutyn ende.

In couplets.

62. Of the Resurrection. Arund.285.f.174b. s.xvi.
5 stanzas of 8 lines.

R. Off þe Resurrectioun of crist.

Beg. O Mother of God Inuolat Virgin Mary
Exult in Joy and consolacioun

Ends f.175b. Quhois glaid vprissing blithis euery wycht.

Pr. by Carleton Brown, Religious Lyrics of the XVth Century, pp.177-8.

63. Prose note on the ascension.
Add.37,049.f.81b. s.xv.in.
36 lines.

Beg. Ascendens Cristus in altum dedit dona hominibus þat is cryste ascendyng in to hyght

Ends f.81b. þai sal be juges with oure lord in þe day of dome.

III. THE BLESSED VIRGIN

64. Poem to the Virgin - 'Gaude virgo mater christi' - Lydgate. Harl.2251.f.234b. s.xv.
7 stanzas of 7 lines.

Beg. BE gladde mayde, moder of Jhesu
Whiche conceyvedest only be heryng

Ends f.235. Only of mercy and stynt oure hevynesse.

Other copies, Trinity Camb. 600, p.53; Trinity Camb. 601,f.173a. Pr. by MacCracken, E.E.T.S., E.S.cvii, pp.288-9, from Trinity Camb. 600.

65. Poem to the Virgin - 'Haile, flos campi, O ave, Jesse virgula' - Lydgate.
Harl.2251.f.30b. s.xv.
19 stanzas of 8 lines.

Beg. Haile blissede lady, þe moder of criste Jhesu
Of pees and concorde haile fresshest onlyve

Ends f.32b. That syng of hole herte o Ave Jesse virgula.

Another copy, Trinity Camb. 601,f.163a. Pr. by MacCracken, E.E.T.S., E.S.cvii, pp.299-304, from Harl.2255 f.140 and this MS.

66. Another copy, Harley 2255,f.140 (lacks stanzas 1-7).

67. Poem - 'Quinque Gaudia'. Cotton. Caligula. A.II.f.135.
s.xv.med.
5 stanzas of 8 lines.

R. Quinque Gaudia.

Beg. Heyl gloryous virgyne ground of alle our grace
Heyl moder of crist in pure virginite

Ends f.135. These joyes fyve empryntyng in oure myndes Amen.

Col. Explicit.

Other copies, Bodl. 6943. Cf. MacCracken, Archiv. CXXXI, pp.49-50; pr. by Carleton Brown, Religious Lyrics of the XVth Century, pp.53-4, from this MS.

68. Another copy, Add.17,376,f.198b.

69. Another copy, Add.29,729,f.130b.

70. Poem to the Virgin - 'Ave Regina celorum' - Lydgate. Harl.2251.f.34b. s.xv.
6 stanzas of 8 lines.

Beg. Haile luminary and benynge lanterne
Of Jerusalem the holy orders nyne

Ends f.35. Where more joy is than tunge may telle
Ave regina celorum.

Other copies, Trinity Camb., 601,f.162a and at f.233a. Pr. by MacCracken, E.E.T.S., E.S.cvii, pp.291-2, from Trinity Camb. 601,f.162a.

71. Ave maris stella. Add.37,049.f.27b. s.xv.in.
18 lines.

R. Aue maris stella dei mater alma.

Beg. f.27b. Hayle se sterne gods modyr holy
Pray þu þi swete son safe vs fro foly

Ends.f.27b. Þat we with þe may dwelle for euer & ay Amen.

Nine couplets. With drawing of Christ and the Virgin in Glory. Pr. by Carleton Brown, Religious Lyrics of the XVth Century, pp.35-6. Cf. Brunner, Anglia LXI, pp.145-6.

72. Poem to the Virgin - 'Gaude flore virginale'. Harl.372.f.55. s.xv.
8 stanzas of 8 lines.

R. Gaude flore virginali

Beg. Joy blissid lady with pure virgynal floure
And honoure special transendyng vpon hee

Ends f.55b. And suffir vs neuer to þe fend to mak oure soulys thralle. Amen.

Pr. by Hammerle, Anglia LV. pp.429-30 and by Carleton Brown, Religious Lyrics of the XVth Century, pp.63-5, from this MS.

73. On the name of Mary. Add.37,049.f.26. s.xv.in.
16 lines.

Beg. Luf wele þis blyssed name Maria ffor saynt Bernarde says

Ends if þu will not suffer puttyng bakke.

With two drawings: (i) a tree bearing the word 'Maria' on a decorative scroll and (ii) Christ showing wounds.

74. Poem to the Virgin - Hymn on the 'Regina celi letare' - Lydgate. Harl.2251.f.35b. s.xv.
5 stanzas of 8 lines.

Beg. O thow joieful light, eternel ye shyne
In glory with laureat coronalle

Ends f.36. Banysshede is oure sorw and aduersite
Dicamus omnes alleluya.

Other copies, Trinity Camb. 601,f.162b and at f.233b. Pr. by MacCracken, E.E.T.S., E.S.cvii, pp.293-4, from Trinity Camb. 601,f.162b. Cf. also item 288, and Thurston, Familiar Prayers, pp.150-1.

75. Life of the Virgin Mary - Lydgate.
Cotton, Appendix VIII, f. 2. s. xv.
5,936 lines in rime royal; the Magnificat in 8-line stanzas.

Beg. O thoughtfull herte plunged in distresse
With slumbre of slouthe þis longe wyntris nyght

Ends f. 108. To kepe and saue from alle aduersite.
Amen.

Numerous MSS., cf. Brown and Robbins, Index of ME Verse, item 2574. Pr. by Caxton, c. 1484; Robert Redman, 1531; J. A. Lauritis pr. from Durham Univ. MS Cosin v. ii. 16 in Lydgate, The Life of Our Lady, 1961; Ch.'s 1-23 pr. by C. E. Tame, English Religious Literature, No. 2, London 1879. Ritchie, STS, n. s. XXII. pp. 60-3. the Magnificat only.

Other copies:-

76. Arund. 168, f. 66 (wanting st. 1-59 and ends imperf.)

77. Harl. 629, f. 4b.

78. Harl. 1304, f. 4.

79. Harl. 2382, f. 1. (beg. imperf.)

80. Harl. 3862, f. 1.

81. Harl. 3952, f. 2.

82. Harl. 4011, f. 23.

83. Harl.4260,f.2.

84. Harl.5722,f.1. (beg. imperf.)

85. Sloane 1785,f.14. (beg. and ends imperf.)

86. Add.19,252,f.4. (beg. and ends imperf.)

87. Add.19,452,f.2. (beg. and ends imperf.)

88. Add.29,729,f.122 (Magnificat only)

89. Prose tract on the Blessed Virgin.
Add.37,049.f.21. s.xv.
53 lines.

R. Of þe fayrnes of saynt Mary gods moder our lady.

Begins f.21. Oof þe fayrhed of saynt Mary Alexander says þat thre fayrenesses is one is natural ane oþer is spryitual þe thyrd is essencyal [sic].

Ends f.21b. And wher þe holy gost is þis þe holy tryhyte indyuysibill inapprehensybyll o god almyghty.

Accompanied by drawing of the Virgin and Child.

90. Poem on the Virgin - 'Gloria dicta sunt de Te' - Lydgate. Harl.2255.f.135. s.xv.
29 stanzas of 8 lines.

Beg. On hooly hillys, moost famous of Renoun
Reysed on hayghte from the valeys lowe

Ends f.139b. Ther gloryous thynges be seid and songe of the.

Col. Explicit quod lydgate.

Another copy, Trinity Camb. 600,p.l. Pr. by MacCracken, E.E.T.S., E.S.cvii, pp.315-23 from the Trinity Camb. MS.

91. Another copy, Harley 2251,f.239.

92. Another copy, Add.29,729,f.146b.

93. Another copy, Add.34,360,f.57.

94. St. Jerome on the life of the Blessed Virgin. Harl.2339.f.13b. s.xv.
17 lines to page.

R. Here eendiþ þe reuelacioun & bigynneþ þe Writynge of Seynt Jerom.

Beg. SEynt Jerom writiþ of hir liif on þis wise

Ends f.16. if it be þi wille. Amen.

Col. Explicit.

95. Poem to the Virgin - 'Veni coronaberis'.
Cotton. Caligula A.II.f.107b. s.xv.med.
9 stanzas of 8 lines.

Beg. Surge me sponsa so swete in syȝte
And se þy sone in sete fulle shene

Ends f.108. Thus enþeth sic [þis] songe of gret swettenesse
Veni coronaberis.

Col. Explicit.

Another copy, Lambeth 853, p.1. Pr. by Carleton Brown, Religious Lyrics of the XVth Century, pp.65-7, from this MS.; and by Furnivall, E.E.T.S., O.S.24, pp.1-3, from the Lambeth MS.

96. Another copy, Harley 2251,f.18a.

97. Stella celi extirpavit - attributed to Lydgate. Add.34,360.f.68b. s.xv.ex.
4 stanzas of 8 lines.

R. Stella celi extirpauit.

Beg. Thow heuenly qwene of grace oure lodesterre
With thi chast mylk plentewus of plesaunce

Ends f.69. Save al thy seruauntis from stroke of pestilence.

Other copies, Jesus Camb. 56,f.73a; Trinity Camb. 601,f.168b; Chetham (Manchester) 6709,f.283a (seven stanzas). Pr. by Carleton Brown, Religious Lyrics of the XVth Century, pp.208-10, from the Chetham MS.

98. Another copy, Harley 2251,f.9b.

99. Another copy, Harley 2255,f.103a.

100. Lamentation of Our Lady.
Cotton. Cleopatra. D.VII.f.183. s.xv.
32 lines to page.

R. Here begynneth the Lamentacioun of oure lady seint Marie And alle the wordes of substance that weryn y spoke betwene Jhesu hir sone and her in tyme of his passion.

Beg. Whan I Marie Jhesu moder sat in Jerusalem in the holy fest of Esterne aloone

Ends f.187b. we were rathere with sorowe y blessede be my swete sone Jhesu.

Col. And thus endeth the Lamentacioun of our lady seint marie Amen Amen.

101. Plaint of the Blessed Virgin - Lydgate. Harl.2251.f.42b. s.xv.
19 stanzas of 8 lines.

Beg. Who shal gyve vnto my hede a welle
Of bitter teeris my sorw to compleyne

Ends f.44b. That for theyr love was naylede to a tre.

Other copies, Bodl. 798,f.78a; St. John's Oxf. 56, f.73b; Jesus Camb. 56,f.19b. Pr. by MacCracken, E.E.T.S., E.S.cvii, pp.324-9, from the Bodley MS.

102. Another copy, Harley 2255,f.66b.

103. Contemplation on the Joys of Our Lady. Harley 494.f.85b. s.xv.
19 lines to page.

R. Contemplacioun for the ffeste of þe assumpcioun of owre blessid ladye.

Beg. The first singlere joye þat sche had was when the angelle gabrielle

Ends f.87b. and in euer yche of the materes a supplicacioun.

104. Poem on the Five Joys of the Virgin - Lydgate. Harl.2255.f.111b. s.xv.
10 stanzas of 8 lines, the last of 4.

R. Incipit de sancta maria.

Beg. O Queen of heuene, of helle Eek emperesse
lady of this world O verray lood sterre

Ends f.113b. To make you stronge bewar forget hem nouht.

Col. Explicit quod lidgate.

Other copies, Bodl. 798,f.17a; Bodl. 1475; Bodl. 4119,f.119b; Bodl. 9336,f.241a and at f.244a; Bodl.11914,f.80a; Camb. Univ. Kk.1.6.f.199a; Jesus Camb. 56,f.71b; Trinity Camb. 601,f.167b; Lambeth 344,f.11a. Pr. by MacCracken, E.E.T.S. E.S.cvii, pp.284-7, from Bodl. 9336,f.244a.

105. Fifteen Joys of Our Lady - Lydgate. Cotton. Titus A.XXVI.f.157b. s.xv.
28 stanzas of 7 lines.

R. To my lordes and ladyes here Begynnen þe fyfftene Joyes of oure lady cleped þe xv. Ooes translated oute of frenshe into Englisshe by dann John the Monke of Bury at þinstance of þe worshipfulle Pryncesse Isabelle nowe Countasse of Warr.

Beg. Blessed lady O Pryncesse of mercy
Moder ecallyd of grace and of pyte

Ends f.160b. And my sovle to save whane I schale hence wende. Amen.

Other copies, Trinity Camb. 601,f.170a; Phillipps 8820, art.4. Pr. by MacCracken, E.E.T.S., E.S. cvii, pp.260-7, from this MS.

106. The Fifteen Joys of Our Lady.
Add.37,049.f.68. s.xv.in.
41 lines.

Beg.f.68. Þe tent ioy had our lady at þe feste of
Architriclyne
When our lord Jhesu tarned water into wyne

Ends f.68 Þat we may reyne euer with hym
withouten ende Amen.

In couplets. Imperf. at beginning.

107. Poem on the Annunciation - 'Missus est angelus Gabriel'. Royal 18 A X.f.123b. s.xv.in.
19 stanzas of 4 lines.

Beg. God sent hys aungell Gabriell
To Nazareth þe chefe cite

Ends f.124b. Seynt Johan Baptist fro schame vs
schilde. Amen.

Pr. by W. Sandys, Christmas Carols, no.7.

108. Poem on the Assumption - 'Maria Virgo assumpta est'. Harl.2251.f.33. s.xv.
10 stanzas of 8 lines, the 1st and 8th of 7.

Beg. REgina celi, qwene of thy [sic] sowth
A fourmed by Salamon his sapience

Ends f.34. That she may comfort vs in al oure fere
Maria virgo assumpta est.

Pr. by MacCracken, Archiv. CXXXI, pp.50-1.

IV. PERSONAL VISIONS, ETC.

109. Meditations ascribed to St. Ambrose. Harl.535.f.117. s.xv.
23 lines to page.

1. Beg. Whan þou schapist þe to pray or to haue eny deuocioun: fonde to haue a priuey place fram al manere noyse

   Ends f.118. þei hym leeued almost for deed.

2. R. Compassio sancte marie.

   Beg.f.118. LOke þanne a side uppon his blessid moder Se what sorowe sche makiþ

   Ends f.121. departid fram þe body in paynes of purgatorye abidyng þy mercy. Amen.

3. Beg.f.121. My lyf makeþ me agast & agryse

   Ends f.125. regnyst for euere wiþouten ende. Amen.

4. Beg.f.125. My soule mescheuous soule þou wrecchid soule

   Ends f.129b. To þee be heryyng, praysyng, worschip & ioye wiþ outen ende. Amen. Amen. Amen.

5. Beg.f.129b. CRistyne soule. arerd from dedlich slepe

   Ends f.137b. þou hire haue for euere þat art y blessid with outen ende. Amen.

6. Beg.f.137b. LOrd Jhesu crist my raunsum. my mercy

   Ends f.142. in heuene trone in his glorye euerlastyng. Amen.

   Col. Explicuit meditaciones sancti Ambrosii.

110. Vision of St. Anthony. Add.37,049.f.75b. s.xv.in.
23 lines.

Beg. Opon a nyght a voyce come to saynt Anton and sayd

Ends f.75b. þorow þe myght of god sal owen þe deuell.

With a drawing.

111. Meditations of St. Bernard.
Royal. 17 C.XVII.f.89b. s.xv.
33 lines to page.

R. Here begynnith the blissed meditacions of the holy doctor seynt Barnerde.

Beg. Many know many thyngis and know not hemselfe, othir thei beholde

Ends f.104b. god of glorie that livith and reygneth withowten ende. Amen.

Attributed both to St. Bernard and Hugo de S. Victore. Not the same translation as that pr. by W. de Worde, The Meditations of Saint Bernard, 1496.

112. Revelations of St. Birgitta.
Cotton. Julius. F.II.f.1. s.xv.
27 lines to page.

Beg. WOndyr and mervelys are herd in owre cuntre and in owre londe

Ends f.246b. with gret deuocion and reuerens she gaf hit sprich among the persones be here seyde.

Col. The last heuenly booke of reuelaciouns of blissid brigid princes of Nerice of the kingedom of Swecy is endid. Amen. Deo gracias.

Cf. W.P. Cumming, The Revelations of Saint Birgitta (E.E.T.S., O.S.178, 1929) from a Princeton Univ. MS. Other copies, Bodley MS. Rawlinson C.41; Lambeth MS.432. On St. Birgitta, cf. Acta Sanctorum, Oct. t.IV, pp.368-560; Analecta Bollandiana, T.12 (1893), p.325; T. Höjer, Studier i Vadstena klosters och Birgittinordens historia intel midten of 1400-talet, (Uppsala, 1905).

113. Another copy. Cotton. Claudius B I.f.5. s.xv.

Beg. imperf. (commencing in the middle of ch.1)
Of man þat I have boght with mine owen blode

Last three chapters of Book VII missing.

114. Another copy. Harley 4800.f.1. s.xv.

Consists of Book IV and the beginning of Book V only.

Beg. A persone appered to þe spouse semynge to her

Ends f.109b. Therfor ho þat forsaketh hys propre wyl and ys obedient to me he schal have hevyn wythoute peyne.

115. Another copy, Arundel 197.f.38b. s.xv.

(Book VI. ch.65 and Book II. ch.16.)

116. Short note on the Visions of St. Bridget. Add.37,790.f.236b. s.xv.med.
30 lines.

Beg. God Almyghty Apered to Seynte Bryde sayinge to hir on this wyse, doughter he sayde

Ends f.236b. þat þu trauell in fastyngye in wakyngye & in prayers & oþer goode dedys for all

Imperf., owing to the cutting out of f.237.

117. Treatise concerning St. Bridgit's Vision of the Number of Christ's Wounds.
Harl.172.f.3b. s.xv.

Beg. HEre beginnythe a tretyse of a solytarye and a recluse woman she covetynge to knowe the noumbre of the wondys of oure lord Jhesu cryste oftynetymes she prayede

Ends.f.5b. Hit ys seyde and tolde that thys womans Name was Seynt Bryde that fulle many reuelacyons and grete graces she hadde of oure lorde Jhesu cryste.

118. Tract on a Vision of St. Bridgit.
Harley 494.f.88b. s.xv.
19 lines to page.

Beg. Oure lady apperid to seynt Brigitt & seyd I am the quene of heuen and thou art studious & desirous to know

Ends f.89b. Good lord haue mercy on me for her prayers.

119. Julian of Norwich - Revelations of Divine Love. Add.37.790.f.97. dated 1413
32 lines to page.

R. Here es A Visioun Schewed Be the goodenes of God to A deuoute Womann and hir Name es Julyan that is recluse atte Norwyche and ȝitt is onn lyfe. Anno domini millesimo CCCCXIII°. In the whilk visyoun er fulle many comfortabylle wordes and gretly Styrrande to alle thaye that desyres to be crystes looverse.

Beg. I desyrede thre graces be the gyfte of god. The ffyrst was to have mynde of Cryste es Passioun

Ends f.115. peessabill & ristefull as he is to vs so will he that we be to oure selfe. And to oure Evencristen. Amen.

Col. Explicit Juliane de & Norwych. [sic]

Other copies, Bibl. Nat. Fonds Anglais, No. 40 (s.xvi); Sloane 2499 (s.xvii); Sloane 3705 (s.xviii.in.)

Pr. by Dom Serenus Cressy, sine loco, 1670, (apparently from Bib. Nat. MS.); H. Collins, London, 1877, (based on Dloane 2499, text modernised); Grace Warrack, London, 1901, (based on Sloane 2499); Dundas Harford, London, 1911 (transcription of Add. 37, 790); R. Hudleston, London, 1927 (from Sloane 2499, text modernised); A.M. Reynolds, London, 1958 (from Add.37,790); J. Walsh, London, 1961 (from Paris MS. and Sloane 2499).

Harford (ed.,p.viii) considers that the Add. MS. text, which is considerably shorter than the other texts, is not likely to be a series of extracts since it contains many details not mentioned in the longer version and is 'what might be called the "first edition" of the Revelations', the later version being the outcome of the twenty years subsequent meditation referred to in the last chapters of the longer version. Both Hudleston (p.xi) and Knowles (in The English Mystical Tradition, p.120) accept this view. The scribe of the Add. MS. wrote in 1413, forty years after the date of the revelations and states that Julian was still alive at this time.

120. Lydgate's Testament.
(in five sections). Harl. 2255.f.47. s.xv.
30 stanzas of 8 lines.

R. Testamentum Johann lidgate nobille poete.

Beg. O how holsom and glad is the memorye
Of crist Jhesu surmountyng al swetnesse

Ends f.52. With Jhesu mercy kneelyng on my kne.

Other copies, Bodl. 798,f.88a; Bodl. 11951,f.62b (Pt. 5 only); Jesus Camb. 56,f.1a; Trinity Camb. 599,f.162[a] (Parts 2, 3 and 4), etc.
Pr. by Pynson [1515?], MacCracken, E.E.T.S., E.S. cvii, pp.329-62, from Harley 218; Halliwell, Percy Soc. II. 232-64 from Harley 2255.

Other copies.

121. Arund. 285,f.170b. (Part 5 only).

122. Harl. 218,f.52b.

123. Harl. 2251,f.40. (Part 5 only).

124. Harl. 2382, f.87b-96b, 108-108b, 128b-129b.

125. Royal 18 D. ii.f.1b (lacks Part 1).

126. Add. 29,729.f.179b. (Part 1 only).

127. Add. 34,193, f.223b. (st. 1-44).

128. Visions of Saint Matilda Egerton 2,006. s.xv.
About 33 lines to page.

Ff. 1-20b. contains a list of contents, with summaries of the chapters.

R. Incipit liber sancte Matildie.

Beg. f.20b. Jhesu mercy with drawe nowe thy rodde of ryghtwynes benethe me nought thye grace

Ends f.212. als I sayde in the begynnynge so I saye in the endynge. A Jhesu mercy. Amen.

Col. Explicit liber Sancte Matildis virginis Et Monache.

As printed by Jacobus Faber [Jacques le Fèvre] in his 'Liber trium virorum et trium spiritualium virginum', (Paris, 1513).

129. Ruysbroeck - Treatise of Perfection of the Sons of God - translation into English Add.37,790. s.xv.med.
33 lines to page.

R. In the Name Off The Blissid Trinite In Whomm at all tymes I putt my dispocicoun and werks, I intende to transpose for myne owne lernynge A trettese frome latynn in to Englysch compiled bi Dan John Rusbroke the ffirst Prior of the

Chartyr howse in valle viridi iuxta bruxellam Whichetretysse is called the tretesse of perfeccioun of the Sonnys of god that es to saye the grownde and the ledere Vnto the trew wayse of perfeccioun Wherfore ȝif ony man happenn to rede it or ȝit here it redde whiche Approbately can defete it Mekely I beseche þame to withdrawe the defawte and gyffe stede to the trowthe And att my begynnynge be mary the blyssed virgynn and so forthe procedynge vnto the ende. Amen.
Explicit prologus. Here begynnes a trettesse the which es called the trettesse of perfeccioun Off the Sonnys Of God. Deo gracias.

Beg. Who so euer will lyffe in the moste perfytt state of the moder holy chirche

Ends f.130. gyffe tha me grace that this trettesse schalle rede trewly and charetabely to consayfe & reporte & euer to praye for þe writer whilke graunt Jhesu Domini.

Col. Explicit the tretyse of perfeccioun Off the sonnes of god conteynynge xvi chapitures to man sawle ryght be hofulle and necessary. Jhesu mercy. Deo gracias.

Anonymous translation into English of the Latin version (by William Jordaens?) of Jan van Ruysbroeck's work in Flemish 'Dat Hantvingherlijn oft van den Blickenden Steene'.

130. The Mirror of Simple Souls.

Add.37,790.f.137. s.xv.med.
28 lines to page.

R. To the Worschyp and lawde Off Trinite be þis worke begunne and endid. Amen. The prologe

Prologue beg. This boke the which is called þe myrroure of Symple Saules, I moste vnworthy creature and oute cast of alle

Prologue ends f.138b. that they wolle vowche safe to correcte and amende þem that I do amys.

Col. Here endith þe prologe of the translator that drewe this booke out of ffrensch into englisch And here Begynnes the Prologe in two chapiters vpon the same booke that loue & sameth the myrrour of Simple saules. Oure lorde god crist Jhesu bringe it to a goode ende Amen.

Text beg. I Creature made of the makere bi me that the makere hase made of hym this boke

Ends f.225. Therfore his eyȝ behaldes me þat he loues none mare than me nowe. Amen.

Col. Here endeth the Boke That Loue calles the myrroure Off Symple Saules. Who that this booke wille vndirstande Take þat lorde to his Spouse louande That is god in Trinite. Jhesu mercy and grace Marie Praye ffor vs. Endren desormes. M. N. Siȝhe and sorowe deepelie morne and wepe ynwardlie Pray and thenke deuoutly Loue and longe contynnely.

English version of an unidentified French mystical work, mainly in the form of a dialogue between Reason and Love. The translator in his preface gives his initials as M.N., which he uses to mark the beginning and end of his own insertions in the text.

Other copies, Bodl. 505; St. John's Coll. Camb. 71. A Latin translation made from the English version by Richard Methley of Mount Grace is in Pembroke Coll. Camb. MS.221. The 13th-century French original is not known. All the English MSS. are mid-15th century.

Pr. by Clare Kirchberger, The Mirror of Simple Souls, (London, 1928), with modernised text, based on the Bodley MS., collated with the BM and both the English and Latin Cambridge MSS. Other Latin translations, made from the lost French original, are stated by Kirchberger to exist in the Vatican Library.

131. <u>Poem on 'Jesus Nazarenus' with a prose note</u> - an exhortation to prayer.
<u>Add.37,049</u>. s.xv.
8 lines verse,
29 lines prose.

R. iehus nazarenus [in large ornamented letters].

Begs f.23b. Our lord Jhesu crist dyd appere
To saynt Edmunde þe archebischop clere

Ends f.23b. Þerto hym god his grace dyd graunte
& also to oþer þat wil þis writtyng haunte.

Prose note begins f.23b. It is written þat þer was in gret paynes a saule þe whilk a monke saw in vision

Ends f.24. And þan þai opynd his syde & sawe it so & in his hert þai fande written Amor meus Jhesu. Jhesu is my luf.

132. <u>Jesus est amor meus</u>. <u>Add.37,049.</u>f.36b. s.xv.in.
45 lines.

R. Jhesu est amor meus [in a drawing of the Crucifixion].

Beg.f.36b. Þe luf of god who so will lere
In his hert þe name of Jhesu he bere

Ends f.36b. And fest þi luf into my þoght
So þat we non more twyn. Amen.

Pr. by Comper, <u>Spiritual Songs</u>, pp.133-4, from this MS.

133. <u>Jhesu est amor meus</u>. <u>Add.37,049</u>.f.37. s.xv.in.
52 lines.

R. Jhesu est amor meus [on a scroll in a drawing of the Crucifixion and Christ in Glory].

Preface

Beg.f.37. Whils I satte in a chapel in my prayere
A heuenly sonde to me drewe nere

Ends f.37. And nayled on a tre þe bright angels brede.

Poem

Beg. f.37. I knaw no þinge þat so inwardly þi luf to god wyl brynge
As of cristes passion & deth deuoute þinkinge

Ends f.37. Deuoutely in Jhesu ȝour hertes ȝe caste.

Another version of poem on f.36b. Both these are translations of Rolle's <u>Incendium Amoris</u>, XV.189. No other copies exist. Pr. by Comper, <u>Life and Lyrics of Rolle</u>, p.315; Comper, <u>Spiritual Songs</u>, pp.209-10, from this MS.

V. THE CHRISTIAN LIFE, ETC.

i. GENERAL.

134. The Apple of Solace.
Add.37,049.f.69b. s.xv.in.
46 lines to page.

Beg. f.69b. Now gode angel telle me what ȝondyr pepyl menes þat plays & has þair solace with ȝon appyll

Ends f.70. Always be he fest in þi mynde þat ones for þe was fest þe cros.

Prose tract on charity and divine understanding, etc.

135. Short extract, with quotations from St. Augustine. Add.37,790.f.236. s.xv.med.
26 lines.

Beg. LAbure hastely for the tyme is schorte and considyr Austynn that says

Ends f.236b. As who say he has more compassioun of a synner than a synner can haue of hym selfe.

136. Christ's words to St. Moll.
Harley. 4012.f.77b. s.xv.
39 lines.

R. Theis be the wordis that our saueoure Jhesu spake to his holy spouse and virgen Sent Molle in al thi werkes kepe iij thingis in thi mynde.

Beg. Oone is what seruice or benefice or humanite be donne vnto þe

Ends f.78. That blisse he us graunt þat is endles god in trinite Amen.

137. De contemptu mundi. Add.37,049.f.35b. s.xv.in. 41 lines.

R. Note þis wele of dispisyng of þe warld.

Beg. f.35b. Werely I knawe no þinge þat so inwardly sal take þi hert to couet gods luf

Ends f.35b. bot only þinkyng of god & of þe fayrhed of angels & hely saules.

138. Formula compendiosa vite spiritualis. Add.37,790.f.135b. s.xv.med. 43 lines to page.

R. fformula compendiosa vite Spiritualis.

Beg. In the felaschippe of sayntis whilke as þe morne sterne schone

Ends f.136b. fle kepe sylence and be in reste Thise he sayde ar the principles of gostely hele. Deo gracias.

Part of ch.iv of the English abridged version of the Horologium Sapientiae (in the Latin, lib. ii, cap.iii), which is itself translated from the German of Henricus de Suso. Not the same version as that printed by Horstmann, Anglia, X, p.353.

139. Another copy, Add.37,049.f.43b. s.xv.in.

140. Extract from the 'Horologium Sapientiae' Ch.v. Add.37,049.f.39. s.xv.in.
46 lines to page.

R. It is written in þe boke þat is cald horologium diuine sapien how a man sal lerne for to dye & desyre for to dye for þe luf of Jhesu lyke as ȝe may fynde here fylowyng [sic].

Beg. f.39. Sen it is so þat deth gyfes not to man bot rather takes fro hym of þat he has

Ends f.43b. so þat þu may cum at þe laste to þe place of immortalite vndedlynes & euerlastyng felicite & hapynes Amen.

With drawings. Chapter v. of the English abridged version of the dialogue Horologium Sapientiae (usually attributed to Jehan de Soushauie in the French version, e.g. Harl.MS. 4386), in the original lib.ii. cap.ii. A version in a different dialect pr. from a Douce MS. by Horstmann, Anglia x, p.357. The Latin original, by the Dominican St. Amandus (Heinrich von Berg al. von Seuss) has been printed (Venice, 1492, etc.)

141. Another copy, Harley 1706.f.20.

142. The life of soul. Arund.286.f.115. s.xv.
29 lines to page.

R. Here begynneþ a tretis þat is depiit þe lyfe of soule secundum doctores.

Beg. Dere fader as seynt paule seiþ we haue here no cytee þat is dwellynge

Ends f.129. And god graunt þat we so doo. Amen. Amen. Amen.

Treatise on the Christian life with discussion of hard points in Scripture and the Vices and Virtues.

143. The state of religion.
Add.37,049.f.37b. s.xv.in.
90 lines.

R. Of þe state of religion.

Beg.f.37b. Þe state of religioune suld be þorow right intencione ffar fro þe warld as þe boke telles

Ends f.38. And hafe hym þan for euermare. Amen.

Imperf. In 45 couplets, with drawings of 'the mount of perfection' (figures kneeling at the foot of a ladder whose rungs are 'meknes, pouerte, obediens, chastite and charite', and at the top, Christ with saints in Glory) and of the tree of religion.

144. Templum Domini. Add.32,578.f.105b. s.xv.
In 4 line stanzas,
784 lines.

R. Incipit templum domini.

Beg. Gode þat all thynges first began
Has giffen his grace in diuerse gyse

Ends f.116. Als he of noȝt alle thynges begann
Gif vs þe blisse þat lastes ay.

Col. Explicit templum domini.

An English trans. of Grossteste's treatise, Templum Domini. Much of the poem is a moral treatise on the Christian life. Cf. Roberta Cornelius, The Figurative Castle, (Bryn Mawr 1930), pp.91-112.

145. Poem on the ways of the world.
Add.37,049.f.72. s.xv.in.
56 lines

Beg. f.72. Alle þe warld wyde & brade
Oure lord specyally for man made

Ends f.72. .... wretchyd warld as ye may se

Imperf., last line cut off. In couplets.

146. Apostolus dicit Ciuitatem hic manentem non habemus. Add.37,049.f.36. s.xv.in.
46 lines.

R. Apostolus dicit Ciuitatem hic manentem non habemus.

Beg.f.36. Behold how in þe wilderness of þis warld men gase
Bot þerin place of abydynge none hase

Ends f.36. Þat þai go not to payne withouten ende.

In 23 couplets. Accompanied by the common Vado Mori device, three figures, a king, bishop and knight each with a scroll with verses.

147. Treatise on the Christian's Warfare. Arund.286.f.20. s.xv.
23 lines to page.

R. Milicia cristi Induite uos armatura dei ut pollitis stare aduersus insidias diabolij. ad ephesios g°. Þes beþ þe wordys of seynt paule þe apostel ...

Ends f.81b. and saluacoun & helpe to me to lyfe & to soule & to alle men & wymmen enemyes & frendes Amen.

Semi-allegorical treatise likening Christian virtues to items of a knight's armour; additional material concerning 'points of belief' on the Incarnation, the Sacrament of the Altar, the Trinity.

148. Treatise on Humility.
Royal 17 C.XVIII. s.xv.
33 lines to page.

R. Here begynneth þe tretyse of xii degrees of mekenes.

Beg. Seynt Gregor the doctour seith that withouten mekenes itt is vnlefull

Ends f.82. itt semyth in the louynge of godd.

149. Another copy, Harley 4011,f.16.

150. Another copy, Harley 4012,f.79.

151. Of the seven Degrees of Humility, according to Seynt Anselme.
Harl.1706.f.94b. s.xv.
36 lines.

R. Seynt Anselme seyth as redeth in a booke of contemplacioun that ther be vij degrees of humylyte

Beg. The ffirst degre of mekenes ys a man to knowe hym selfe that he ys wreched

Ends f.94b. sekyng after no mede nor praysyng but only of god.

152. Four tokens of love. Royal 18 **A.**X.f.15. s.xv.in.
30 lines to page.

R. Fowre tokenis of loue.

Beg. Tokenes ther ben foure, whether thu loue god in charite

Ends f.15. Si sis de dignis hiis quatuor accipe signis audi, plange, caue, fac, te deus eruet a ve.

153. How to love God. Harl.2339.f.72b. s.xv.
17 lines to page.

R. And here sueþ anoþir mater how ech man & womman may lerne to love & serue God ech in his degree takynge ensaumple bi þre foolis

Beg. Biholde ȝe þe foulis of heuene for bi hem may men lerne

Ends f.78. ouer al þing in þis world.

154. Relations of God to Man.
Royal 18 A.X. s.xv.
30 lines to page.

Beginning of work wanting. Begins apparently in Capm.iii.

MS. begins f.1. Lefte we vp oure hertes first to Jhesu þat stabley mennes hertes preying hym and be sechyng to telle vs how we mowe come to þis loue

'Capitulum quartum' begins f.1.l.30. Now per auenture þu askes me where þis hows is þat I speke of

155. The Weye to Paradys. Harl.1671.f.1. s.xv.

Beg. imperf., in first chapter of that he hath wratthed hym thorew his mysdede

Ends imperf., f.85b. Where of that he may do hyt in goode maner

Imperf. Prose treatise, frequently citing Robert de Sorbonne.

156. Treatise on the Way of Perfection.
Harley 494.f.6. s.xv.
18 lines to page.

Beg. The gret cause as I do thynke wherfore we profyt lytelle in the way of perfecioun ys that we do not with alle oure study & diligence

Ends f.20. to whom be alle prayse honour & glory without ende. Amen.

157. Of the Seven Degrees of Pride.
Harl.1706.f.94b. s.xv.
24 lines.

R. Ther ben vij degres of pryde.

Beg. The ffirst degre ys a man to holde hym self better than he ys

Ends f.94b. And wolle nat here to be punychede or correctyde as ryght and have wolle Amen

158. Treatise on Prayer and Meditation. Royal. 17 C.XVIII.f.65. s.xv.
33 lines to page.

Beg. Siue manducatis siue bebitis, ... that is to sey whethir ye etyn or drynken

Ends f.77b. gostely desire and sekynge of the godhede.

ii. TRIBULATION.

159. Treatise on tribulation.
Royal 17A. XXV.f.62. s.xv.in.
24 lines to page.

R. Here begynnyth a litil schort tretice that tellyth how þer weren sixe maisters asembliden to gidur and askiden eche oon of oþere what þey myȝte beste speke of that myȝte moost plese god & were moost profitable to þe peple and alle þey weren a cordid to speke of tribulacioun.

Beg. [T]he friste maistir seyde þat if eni þing hadde be bettir

Ends f.63. and to bringe us to his blis that neuere schal haue eende AMEN

Catalogue states:- 'a very brief tract apparently translated from a Latin text which Bale (Index, ed. Poole, p.3) attributes to Adam Carthusianus, who seems to be the same as the author of the Speculum Spiritualium, sometimes called Henricus Carthusianus (Cf. Royal 7 B.XIV. and Catalogue of the Library of Syon Monastery, ed. Bateson, p.107, note 4).' Other copies, Christ Church Oxf. C. CCX; Univ. College Oxf. CXLII, etc. Pr. by W. de Worde with XII Profytes of Tribulacion, 1530 and by Horstmann among works wrongly attributed to Rolle, Richard Rolle and his followers, p.390.

160. Another copy, Cotton, Cleopatra D VII.f.187b.

161. Another copy, Harley 1706,f.54b.

162. Another copy, Royal 17 C.XVIII.f.1.

163. Treatise on tribulation.

Harl.4012.f.113b. s.xv.
26 lines to page.

R. Here is foling [sic] a short and a frutefull tretes how that ther was assembelid xiii wise men and masters for to declare what meret tribulacion is for manne mekely sufferd.

Beg. The first master sayde that tribulacioun is more vnto man

Ends f.114b. Wher as the trinyte is after the trobilacioun of this worlde cui regnat per omnia Secula Seculorum Amen.

iii. LORD'S PRAYER

164. Meditations on the Lord's Prayer.
Royal. 17 C. XVII.f.90. s.xv.in.
36 lines to page, double-columned.

Beg. Oure fadir þat es in heuen A my wrechyd saule when to þe lykenes of heuen sall þu be made

Ends f.90b. (foot of second column) Wen sall luf be my leche of langyng þat lesys trew treasure þu me teche to lyst þat þe lese es amen amen for charite god lord so motte it be.

Prose and alliterative verse.

iv. AVE MARIA.

165. Meditation on the Ave Maria.
Royal 17 C. XVII.f.91. s.xv.in.
(as item 164)

Beg. Ave maria gracia plena, þat es, hayle mary full of grace And gode lady sen it es so þat þu ert full of grace

Ends f.91b. & mary þe tre & Jhesu þe froyte gyves me grace ȝow to se þer ȝe sytte in a soyte amen amen so mot it be dere lady per charyte.

v. THE MASS.

166. Poem on the Mass.
Royal 17 C.XVII.f.155b. s.xv.in.
281 stanzas of 5 lines.

Beg. Þat blysful barne in Bedlem borne
Þat lete hys brayne be thyrled with thorne

Ends f.166. Þerfor blame me no man.

Another copy, Bodl. 29837,f.139a. Cf. Horstmann, Anglia, 4. (1881), pp.109-138.

167. Meritae Missae - Lydgate.
Cotton MS. Titus A.xxvi.f.154. c.1470.
203 lines.

Beg. f.154. God of hewine, þat shoope Erthe And helle
ȝyf me grace svme word to telle

Ends That we be sawyd at domys daye. Amen.
Explicit meryta mysse.

In couplets. Text slightly imperf.; two lines missing. Pr. by Simmons - 'The Lay Folks Mass Book' (E.E.T.S., 1879). pp.148-154, cf. also p.389.

168. Meditations for the time of the Mass.
Harley 494.f.63. s.xv.
19 lines to page.

R. Meditacouns for tyme of the masse.

Beg. The preste goynge to masse signifieth the sauyour of the worlde

Ends f.75. a thousande tymes for hys gret kyndnesse Amen. finis.

vi. DEATH.

169. Ars Moriendi.   Harl.4011.f.3.   s.xv.

Beg. For as myche as the passage of deth owte of the wrechidnes

Ends f.20b. Sey not an evill word

Imperfect.

170. Of the four last things, or The Cordial.   Sloane 779.f.77b.   1478.
27 lines to page.

Beg. This present present [sic] tretys is deuyded in foure pryncypall parties Off the whiche euery parte conteynyth thre other syngeler parties as in the maner folowynge is shewed.

List of contents follows to foot of f.78.

Prologue begins f.78b. MEmorare nouissima & in eternum non peccabis. Ecclestiasticus saith in his vijth chapitre these wordes folowynge

Ends f.79. this present traittye may be entitled & bere the name of the cordyall.

Text proper begins f.79b. I say þat recordynge the remembrance of deth makeþ a man to be meke & humble himself

Ends f.151. the holy goost reignynge in vnyte sempiternally world wtout ende.

Col. of 18 lines, f.151-151b., records date of completion of translation from the French as 'In the xix yere of the Regne of kynge Edward the fourth'.

Ends Laus tibi sit christe gnomam liber explicit iste. Quod Dominus Erace & constast [sic] dane Margaret Wodward.

171. Poem - 'O mors quam amara est memoria tua' - an elegy for the tomb of Lord Cromwell, c.1450.
Cotton. Caligula. A II.f.57b. s.xv.med.
7 stanzas of 8 lines.

R. O mors quam amara est memoria tua.

Beg. O deth howe byttere ys þe mynde of the
That meuere art of mornyng & mone [sic]

Ends f.58. And send vs pees yn perpetuyte.

Pr. by Carleton Brown, Religious Lyrics of the XVth Century, pp.243-5, from the Harley MS.

172. Another copy, Harley 116,f.152b (in 8 stanzas).

vii. DIALOGUES. (1)

173. Dialogue between the Body and the Soul. Royal. 18 A.X.f.61b. s.xv.in.
67 stanzas of 8 lines.

R. A disputeson betwen the body and the sowle.

Beg. As I lay in a wynter nyght
A litel drouknynge befor þe day

Ends f.66b. Þou grante vs for þyn holy grace.
Amen.

Col. Explicit disputacio inter corpus & animam.

Pr. from this MS. by H. Varnhagen, Anglia,ii, 1879, p.229. Cf. four other texts pr. by W. Linow in Varnhagen's Erlanger Beiträge, Heft i, 1889.

---

(1) See also items 195-8.

174. *A disputacion betwixt the body and wormes.* Add.37,049.f.33. s.xv.in.
31 stanzas of 7 lines.

R. A disputacioun betwyx þe body & wormes.

Beg. In þe ceson of huge mortalite
Of sondre disseses with þe pestilence

Ends f.35. Oure saueour & to hym vs bynde. Amen.

Preceded, f.32b, by a drawing with 10 lines of explanatory verse, beg. 'Take hede vn to my figure here abowne'. Accompanied by five drawings of the Crucifixion, Danse Macabre figures, etc. Cf. Brunner, *Archiv*, CLXVII, pp.30-35.

175. *Part of a dialogue between the soul and an angel.* Add.37,049.f.73b s.xv.in.
45 lines.

R. Cut off in binding, traces of a few letters remain.

Beg. Nowe gode angel telle me whedyr þe fende þat has so gret delyte to dysceyfe

Ends f.73b. þat þai w^{t} þe fendys be pyned in torment & payne perdurabyl euerlastyngly.

With two drawings.

176. *Disputation between the soul and the body* - prose dialogue.
Add.37,049.f.82. s.xv.in.
44 lines to page.

R. [Remains of a line of Latin, cut off in binding]. A dysputacion betwyx þe saule & þe body when it is past oute of þe body.

Beg. Þe saule sayd to þe body þus Art þu þere

Ends f.84. & þan sal þai bothe be gloryfyed to geder in euerlastyng ioy.

With drawings.
Cf. Wells, *Manual of Writings in Middle English*, p.411.

viii. JUDGEMENT.

177. Meditation or prayer on the Last Judgement. Add.37,049.f.16b. s.xv. 80 lines in all.

Begins f.16b. Almyghty god for þi gret godenes have mercy of cristen pepyll and graunte þaim grace to stande strongly in þe trewe fayth

Ends f.18. withouten þai hafe grace of amendment or þai dye sal go into euerlastyng fyre fro þe whilk our mercyful lord Jhesu crist þat shed his blode vpon þe rod & dyed for vs safe vs all Amen.

With drawings.

178. The fifteen Tokyns a-forn þe Doom. Harl.2255.f.117. s.xv. 11 stanzas of 8 lines.

R. The fifftene tokyns a forn the doom.

Beg. As the doctour Sanctus Jeronimus
Which þat knew by inspiracioun

Ends f.118b. Thorough cristes passioun that they may come to blisse.

Col. Explicit.

Pr. by T. Wright, Chester Plays, Shakespeare Soc. 1847. II. pp.222-4; MacCracken, E.E.T.S., E.S. cvii, pp.117-20, from this MS. Cat. gives probable source as the 'Prognosticon futuri Seculi' of Julianus Pomerius, Archbishop of Toledo, who died A.D.690.

179. On the Judgement. Add.37,049.f.69. s.xv.in.
46 lines.

R. In omnibus operibus tuis memorare nouissima tua et in eternum non peccaberis.

Beg. f.69. Þat is on ynglysche þus to say
he sayd thynke on þine endyng daye

Ends f.69. Wher euer is day & neuer nyght.

With a drawing.

180. Poem on the Judgement. Add.37,049.f.18. s.xv.
22 lines in all.

R. Of the cumym [sic] of the day of dom.

Begins f.18. The ordyr of þe dome sal be swylk. In þe day of dome oure lorde cumyng to þe dome fyre sal go before hym

Ends f.18b. noȝt with mofyng & trobyll bot by mynysterynge of þoes thynges þe whilk þai sal se before þe day of dome.

181. Poem on the Day of Judgement - 'Non est vestrum nosse tempora'.
Add.37,049.f.18b. s.xv.
42 lines in all.

Begins f.18b. When þe day of dome salle be
It is in gods pryuyte

Ends f.18b. Þerfore gracius god þat alle goodenes hasse
Gyf vs þi mercy here or we passe hence (last word surrounded by ornamental device).

ix. HEAVEN.

182. The Joys of Heaven. Add.37,049.f.80b. s.xv.in.
40 lines, in couplets.

Beg. Behald man & þi þoght vp lede
To heuen with al þi spede

Ends f.80b. ffor þat ioy to hafe and god to se.

183. The Joys of Heaven - Hoccleve.
Royal 17 D.VI.f.137. s.xv.in.

Beg. Loo this is seide of that citee in þat place

Ends f.138b. god of his infynyt goodnesse graunte vs all to cheese. Amen.

Prose conclusion of Hoccleve's 'Lerne to Die', in verse. Pr. by Furnivall, 'Hoccleve's Minor Poems, pt. 1' (E.E.T.S., E.S.lxi, 1892), pp.213-5 from Durham MS. III.9.

x. PURGATORY.

184. Of the relief of souls in Purgatory. Add.37,049.f.24b. s.xv.in.
30 lines (15 couplets).

Beg.f.24b. Þe saules þat to purgatory wendes
May be relefyd þorow help of frendes

Ends f.24b. Her may ȝe se pardon more worthy to gresse
Þan is al warldly rytches.

With drawing of souls being raised from purgatory into Heaven by 'prayer & almos dede'.

xi. HELL.

185. On a vision of hell. Add.37,049.f.74. s.xv.in.
9 stanzas of 4 lines, interspersed with prose.

Prose part begins: Here folowes a vysion of saules þat war dampned. 12 lines of prose.

Verse begins f.74. Cum folow me my frendes vnto helle
Ay to dwelle in helle depe

Ends f.74. Mo þan hert can þinke fer or nere. 36 lines of verse.

With a drawing.

186. A question of the pains of hell. Add.10,036. s.xv.
24 lines to page.

R. A questioun of þe peynes of helle & how soules desireþ to haue rest in þat place.

Begins f.81. Poule & myȝel praied to oure lord Jhesu crist of his gret grace to schewe þe peynes to his disciple poule þat he myȝt declare hem in menyng to cristen peple.

Ends f.85. And þis to euery man hadde foure tounges of Iren ne myȝt nouȝt telle how fele sorwes þer ben in helle. and so sodeynliche þei wente fro þat place.

Pr. in Englische Studien, xxii, p.134.

xii. ANGELS.

187. Songs of the angels. Add.37049.f.70b. s.xv.in.
124 lines.

R. Þies sygnyfies þe saules þat aftyr þair jugement & delyuerance oute of purgatory went vnto blysse with a ful ioyful toyne euer ylk one of þaim more schynyng þan is þe son at mydday hafyng w^t þaim ilkone hys angel þat ledde hym And þis was þe nobyl sange þat þai sange.

Beg. f.70b. Honourd be blyssed lord on hy
Þat of þe blyssed mayndyn was borne.

Ends f.71b. Of þe blissed lord in trynyte.

In couplets; with drawings of angels and Christ in glory. This is the 'Cantus peregrinorum' by Hoccleve, in his English trans. of the Pèlerinage de l'Ame. Pr. by Furnivall, E.E.T.S., E.S. lxxii. pp.xxxii-xxxiii. The Pilgrimage of the Soul was pr. by Caxton in 1483. Other copies: Bodl.2252, f.24a; Corp. Christi Oxf. 237,f.46b; Univ. Coll. Oxf. 181,f.40b; Caius Camb. 124,f.38b; etc.

188. Another copy, Egerton 615,f.102a.

189. Songs of the Angels. Add.37,049.f.76. s.xv.in.

1. Hoccleve - Angels' Song on Epiphany, in Eng. tr. of the Pèlerinage de l'Ame.

R. Þe songe & lofyng of Angels on twelfe day

Beg. Honourd be þis holy feste day
In worschip of þe swete welle of lyfe.

Ends honourd be þe holy trynyte.

4 stanzas of 7 lines.

Other copies, Bodl. 2552,f.94^a; Corp. Christi Oxf. 237,f.127a; Univ. Coll. Oxf. 181,f.143^a; Caius Camb. 124,f.238b. Pr. by Furnivall, E.E.T.S., E.S. lxxii, xlvii-xlviii, from the Egerton MS.

2. R. Þe songe & lofyng of Angels on pase day

   Beg. Honourde be þu Jhesu saueoure
   Þat for man kynde was done on þe rode

   Ends f.76b. honourd be þu blyssed lord Jhesu.

   5 stanzas of 7 lines.

   Same MSS. Pr. by Furnivall, op.cit., xlviii-xlix, from the Egerton MS.

3. R. Þe sang of graces of al holy payntes on pase day

   Beg. Honourd be þu blyssedful lord abof
   Þat vowchest safe þis iornay for to take

   Ends Honourd be þu lord Jhesu suffrayne.

   4 stanzas of 7 lines.

   Same MSS. Pr. by Furnivall, op.cit., p.l.

4. R. Þe songe of angels & oþer payntes on Whyssonday.

   Beg. Honourd be be [sic] þu holy goste in hye
   Þat vn to þe pepyl of so pore estate

   Ends f.77. Honourd be þu lord Jhesu withouten ende.

   With drawings of the Baptism, Resurrection, Christ in majesty, angels, etc. Same MSS. Pr. by Furnivall, op.cit. li.

190. Another copy, Egerton 615,f.99a; etc.

191. Poem on the blessed. Add.37,049.f.74b. s.xv.in. 7 stanzas of 5 lines.

   R. Here is a saule led with myrthe & melody of angels to heuen þe whilk passed vertewosly be þe trewe sacramentes of holy kyrk & kepyng of þe commawndmentes of god oute of þis worlde. Þe sayng of þe angels.

Beg. Honord be þou blyssed Jhesu
And praysed mot þou be in euere place.

Ends f.75. Thankyd be þou Jhesu god & man.

With drawings. Other copies, Bodl. 2552,f.25b; Corp.Christi. Oxf. 237,f.48b; Univ. Coll. Oxf.181, f.43a; Caius Camb. 124,f.42b. Pr. by Furnivall, E.E.T.S., E.S.lxxii, pp.xxxvi-xxxvii, from the Egerton MS. The Angels' Second Song within Heaven, by Hoccleve, in his Eng. tr. of the *Pèlerinage de l'Ame*.

192. Another copy, Egerton 615,f.31a.

193. Tract on angels, etc. Sloane 1009,f.17. s.xv.
32 lines to page.

Beg. We knowyth well by comyn experience that thowe a thynge be neuer so precyouse if þat preciosite be vnknowen

Ends f.28. þu shalte haue þerfore the blisse of hevynn euerlastyng and so be hit Amen.

xiii. MISCELLANEOUS.

194. Poem on a man pursued by a unicorn, representing death.
Add.37,049.f.19b. s.xv.
42 lines in all.

Begins f.19b. Behalde here as þou may se
A man standyng in a tree

Ends f.19b. Imperfect. In gode lyfyng ....
Or fro þis ....
Þu ....

Accompanied by a drawing. Cf. Brunner, *Archiv* CLXVII, p.24.

195. Dialogue between God and Man.
William Lychefelde's 'Complaint of God'.
Add.36,983.f.275. s.xiv.ex.

Beg. Owre gracious god prince of pyte
Whos mi3te whos goodnesse neuer began

Ends f.279b. Þat leuyn synne & hem amende.

Col. Explicit disputacio inter deum et hominem.

Other copies, Corp. Christi, Oxf.237,f.136b:, Camb. Univ. Ff.2.38.f.3a (imperf.); Caius Camb. 174, p.469; Pepys 1584, Art.1; Trinity Camb. 601,f.182a; etc. Pr. by Halliwell, Percy Soc. XIV. pp.87-8; Borgström, Anglia XXXIV, pp.508-25 from the Caius MS; Furnivall, E.E.T.S., O.S.15, pp.198-232 from Lambeth MS. 853. Lychefelde d.1447.

196. Another copy, Harley 2339,f.81b.

197. Another copy, Harley 7333,f.191a.

198. Another copy, Add.36,983,f.275a.

PRAYERS.

I. THE TRINITY AND GOD THE FATHER.

199. Prayer to the Trinity.
Lansdowne 379,f.72b. s.xv.
19 lines to page.

R. Oracio Trinitatis.

Beg. O blessid trinyte fader and sone and holy gost.

Ends f.74. With thy sayntes in blisse withoute ende Amen.

200. Another copy, with slight differences, Cotton. Faustina D IV.f.74b.

201. Prayers to the Trinity and God the Father. etc. Arund.285.f.144. s.xvi.

R. Heir begynnis ane deuoit orisoun to þe Trinite.

a) O Blissit Trinite fathir sone and haly gaist thre personis and ane God I beseik the with myne hert...

Ends f.145. And finalie þat I may cum to þi glore Riall with all þe Sanctis of hevin Amen.

b) f.145. R. Ane orisoun till our lord.

Begins O Lord god almychty all seing all thing knawing

Ends f.145b. And to þe I recommend my saule my faith my life and my dethe Amen

c) Beg. f.145b. R. Ane orisoun till our lord.

MAist deir lord and saluiour sueit Jhesu I beseik þi maist curtes gudnes ...

Ends f.146. And efter in Joy and blis without end sueit Jhesu.

d) Beg. f.146. R. Heir followis ane deuoit orisoun of þe sevin wordis þat our Lord Jhesu said hingand apoun þe croce.

O Lord Jhesu crist þe quilk In thy last life on þe croce ...

Ends f.147 Cum to me and sit with my angellis and Sanctis to Jois and bruke my kinrik be infinit warld of warldes Amen.

e) Beg. f.147. R. Heir followis In Inglis ane deuoit orisoun callit Laus honour et gloria.

O Lord Jhesu crist maist sweit loving honour glor and thank mot be to the

Ends f.147b. And þou grantand þe mortificacioun of my body That I may gif thankis to þe Amen.

f) Beg. f.147b. R. Pater noster.

O Lord Jhesu crist sueit loving honour and glore and thankis be to þe for þe wound of þi left hand

Ends f.147b. and me worthy be thy grace to cum to þi kinrik Amen.

g) Beg. f.147b. R. Pater noster.

F.148.1.1. O Sueit Jhesu loving honour glore and thankis mot be to þe for the wound of þi richt fute

Ends f.148. And leid it to þe eternall Joyis Amen.

h) Beg. f.148. R. Pater noster aue maria

O maist meik Jhesu loving honour glore and thankis be to þe for þat maist haly wound of þi left fute

Ends f.148. And þat I may cum to euerlestand heill with þe anoynting of þi haly oile.

i) Beg. f.148. R. Pater noster aue maria.

F.148b.1.1. O MAist venyng Jhesu loving honour glore and thankis be to the for þe maist haly wound of þi syde

Ends f.148b. þat I may pleis to þe perfitlie here as withoutin end Amen.

j) Beg. f.148b. R. Pater noster aue maria. Ane deuoit orisoun.

O lord Jhesu crist wound my hert with thy haly woundis

Ends f.149b. Loving of the Saluiour of all þe warld Amen.

k) Beg. f.149b. R. Pater noster and Credo Heir followis ane deuoit orisoun to be said in honour of þe wound of þe side of our sueit saluiour Jhesus.

O Thow wound of the syid of our saluiour Jhesu crist

Ends bot þat your mynde be licht in þe sicht of thy godheid Amen.

l) Beg. f.149b. R. Pater noster Aue & Credo Heir followis ane maner of Salutatioun of þe blist woundis of our Saluiour Jhesu. O Thow thankfull heid of crist.

This is followed by a series of seven short prayers to the Five Wounds and the crucified Body of Christ with a concluding prayer to God the Father.

Ends f.150b. And cause our myndis be fervent lufe be in þi haly stinte [sic] Amen.

m) Beg. f.150b. R. Heir followis ane deuoit orisoun till our lord Jhesu Crist callit O Bone Jhesu O dulcis Jhesu.

F.151.1.1. O BONE I H V O meik Jhesu, Jhesu the sone of the virgin mary

Ends f.152. And haue glor in þe euerlestand bliss Amen.

n) Beg. f.152. R. O Rex gloriose Inter Sanctis tuas. O Glorius king amang thy sanctis.

Ends f.152. Now and in tyme euerlestande.

o) Beg. f.152. R. The orisoun in latene callit O gloriose Jesu.

O God quhilk hes maid þe glorius name of þi allanerlit sone

Ends f.152b. þat I mot haue Joy and blithnis without end Amen.

p) Beg. f.152b. R. Heir begynnis in Inglis ane orisone callit deus propicius esto michi ṕeccatory.

O lord God be thow helper to me synnar

Ends f.153. The cross of Crist defend me fra all ewill Amen.

q) Beg. f.153. R. Angelie qui mei est custos.

O Angell that is my keper ordaint

Ends f.153b. gid my dede to þe desire of the maist hie god Amen.

r) Beg. f.153b. R. Ane orisoun to þe proper Angell.

O lord god quhilkis part of thy haly angellis

Ends f.153b. amang þe beistis of his flok Amen.

s) Beg. f.153b. R. O Sancte Angele.

O haly angell quhilk Is þe seruand of þe hevin empir

Ends f.154. honour in warld of warldis That is euerlesting Amen.

t) Beg. f.154. R. Or ȝe gang to confessioun.

O Marcifull god I beseik the for all the orisonis Intercessionis passionis

Ends f.154b. And þat be thy infinit mercy Amen.

u) Beg. f.154b. R. How we aucht to schaw our necessiteis vnto Jhesu crist and ask him grace.

O Richt sueit and maist belouit lord quhilk I now desire

Ends f.155b. Illumyning and lichtling þe vnderstanding of þe creatures.

v) Beg. f.155b. R. Off þe birnyng lufe and gret effectioun þat we suld haue to resaue our saluiour Jhesu crist.

O lord god in souerane deuocioun birnyng lufe

Ends f.157b. you gud lord will haue me pure synnar in rememberance Amen.

w) Beg. f.157b. R. Heir followis ane orisoun callit Conditor coeli.

O lorde god maker of hevin and erðe king of kingis

Ends f.159b. and to pure penitence trew contrition and pure confessioun of all my synnes.

202. Prayer to the Trinity. Add.37,790.f.225b. s.xv.med.
27 lines.

Beg. O Glorious trinite in whom is alle goodnes yhaloued

Ends f.225b. laude preise & magnifie euerlastingly withouten Ende. Amen. Jhesu merci. Amen.

203. Prayer to God. Harley 494.f.96b. s.xv.
19 lines to page.

R. An exclamacioun of a penytent synnere to almighty god for socoure & help knowlegynge hym selff what he is.

Beg. A synfulle wreche a miserable synnere to the þat art fulle of mercy

Ends f.98b. knowest my infirmite better then myselff.

204. Prayer for Mercy. Add.39,574.f.52b. s.xv.in
7 stanzas of
8 lines.

Beg. ALmyȝti God, maker of heuene
Eyr and erþe, watir and wynde

Ends f.53b. Now, Jhesu, þou haue mercy on me. Amen.

Another copy, Camb. Univ. Kk,1.6. Pr. by M. Day, E.E.T.S., O.S.155, pp.67-69 from this MS and by MacCracken, Archiv CXXXI, pp.43-4 from the Cambridge MS.

205. Graces before and after Meat and Supper. Harl.2339.f.121b. s.xv.
34 lines in all.

R. gracis tofore mete.

Beg. Almyȝti god so meritable
In fedinge þou make us resonable

Ends.f.122b. And þat þis bone þus grauntid mai be
Seie we a pater noster & an aue.

Another copy, Trinity Dublin 70,f.194b.

206. <u>On the eight verses revealed to St. Bernard.</u> <u>Royal 17 A.XXVII.f.86b.</u> s.xv.in.

33 lines to page.

R. We redenn in þe lyf of seynt bernard þat þe deuelle seyd to him he knew viii versus in þe sauter þo wheche uersus & a man sey hem wche day he schal neuer be dampnude & seynt bernard askut whiche þey were & he sayde he schulde neuer wyte for hym & he sayde he wolde ellus say þo hol sauter uche day & he answerud & sayd he wold raȝwr telle him whyche þey wer and ȝese hit arne.

Beg. Illumina oculos meos ne umquam obdormiam
ȝyf liȝt unto myn eȝe siȝt
Þat I nouȝt slepe whan I schal dye

Ends f.88b. and me conforte with gostly fode
þat al my lyst be layd on þe.

The eight prayers are each of 8 lines of verse in English, preceded by the first words of the Latin original, viz.

1. Cf. above.
2. In manus tuas domine commendo spiritum meum
   Into þi hondis I be take my gost
3. Locutus sum lingua mea notum fac michi
   I haue spokyn with my tunge
4. Et munierum dierum meorum qui est ut
   and seue þe numbre of dayis inpure
5. Dirupisti uincula mea tibi sacrificabo
   þow hast to broke lord in two
6. Perut fuga a me & non est qui
   fro me haþ fliȝte pischid & failid
7. Clamaui ad te domine deus tu es spes
   I cride & sayde þow art my trist
8. Fac mecum signum in bono ut uideant
   Do with me sum token in gode

Cf. <u>Speculum Spiritualium</u>, f.ccviiib, Add. MS. 33381,f.161. Pr. by Black, <u>Percy Soc</u>. XIX

207. Poem - 'Deus in nomine tuo salvum me fac' - Lydgate.
Cotton. Caligula A II.f.64b. s.xv.med.
9 stanzas of 8 lines.

R. Deus in nomine tuo saluum me fac.

Beg. God in thy name make me safe and sounde
And in thi vertu me deme & justifie

Ends f.65. Hels alle hurt of synnes within tyme and space.

Col. Explicit.

Other copies, Bodl. 6943,ff.69b-70 and 134b. Pr. by MacCracken, E.E.T.S., E.S.cvii, pp.10-12 from this MS; Patterson, The Middle English Penitential Lyric, New York, 1911.

208. Another copy, Harley 116,f.127a.

209. Another copy, Harley 2255,f.146b.

210. Prayer to God. Add.39,574.f.57b. s.xv.in.
2 stanzas of 6 lines.

Beg. GOd, þat madist al þing of nouȝt
And with þi precious blood us bouȝt

Ends f.57b. Mercy for þin holy name.

Pr. by M. Day, E.E.T.S., O.S. 155, p.73 from this MS.

211. Prayers to God.
Cotton. Faustina D.IV.f.77b. s.xv.
24 lines to page.

R. By thes dedes & prayers folowyng a venyalle synnes taken away yf yt be done devowtly [sic]

Beg. In takyng holy water & holy brede also by sayng of the pater noster

Ends f.80. and the souner turne them to goodnesse amen fine deo gracias & marke welle thees verytees.

212. Prayers to God. Harley 494.f.62. s.xv.
16 lines.

Beg. Lorde gode I beseche the that the spirite of strenghth may descende

Ends f.62., imperf. drede & feare when & wher he wyth

213. A series of meditations or prayers. Titus C.XIX.f.3. s.xv.
21 lines to page.

Prol. beg. These Meditacyons or prayers that bene writen with in this boke suwyng bene made to excite and stere the mynde of the reder to the drede of god and to the loue of god and to verey knowyng of hymsilfe

Ends f.4b. be to his worschip and plesyng and oure perpetuall saluacion. Amen.

1. f.5. Myghtfull god that hath in yowe knowyng of me

Ends f.8. to haue and joys your blysse in glorye in heuen wythout ende. Amen.

2. f.8. O ȝe myghtfull god and souerayn lorde Jhesu crist in whom is alle joy and lyfe

Ends f.12b. god infynite þat eternaly schalle dure. Amen.

3. f.12b. O Good lorde myghtfulle god when schalle my gret menableness

Ends f.17b. leues and reynes be euerlastyng worldes. Amen.

4. f.17b. LOrde god ffader of heuen and of erthe to ȝowe I knolyche

Ends f.21b. to euerlastyng joy ther to haue a place.

5. f.21b. O Good lorde god endeles swetnesse of þem þat loues ȝow hertly

Ends f.26. þerfor lorde be to yowe nowe and euer Amen.

6. f.26. O Souerayne god þat suche hath made me as it likyth yowe

Ends f.27b. þat is endeles grete and fayleth to noon þat to 3owe trusteth.

7. f.28. LOrde god pat made me for youre gret goodnes

Ends f.29. and was and euer schalle be wyth outen. Amen. [sic]

8. f.29. O Ryghtfull lorde, gracyous god my fader

Ends f.30b. wyth 3oure delyces so mote it be. Amen.

9. f.30b. O Loue ly3t schynynge ryght clere in bewte

Ends f.33. wyth alle gladnesse mote 3e euer be withouten ende. Amen.

10. f.33. MErcyfulle lorde god almy3ti helpe and amende

Ends f.35. And of verrey contemplacioun. Amen.

11. f.35. O Ryght stronge and ry3t my3tfulle god

Ends f.38b. with enter deuocyons nowe and euer withouten ende. Amen.

12. f.38b. LOrde when 3e wolle temptacions commeth to me

Ends f.40b. leuyth and reyneth wyth outen ende euerlastyng god. Amen.

13. f.40b. O Swete lorde fulle of bry3t3 þat arn my lyght

Ends f.43b. in heuen by youre mercy euer ther to abyde. Amen.

14. f.44. O Pytable god fulle of mercy I þat am youre seruaunte

Ends f.45. euer blessed mote 3e be. Amen.

15. f.45. O Gloryous god my lorde my lyfe and the Illumynacyon of my soule

Ends f.46b. and loue yowe lorde god on hye. Amen.

16. f.47. Almyȝty god of endles lyfe þat arne so full of goodnes

Ends f.48b. in syon þat is in the blysse of heuen. Amen.

17. f.48b. O Swete loue of god þat alle wey brenneth and neuer quenchith

Ends f.50. after youre most plesaunce. Amen.

18. f.50. MOche me owyth and euery man to loue ȝowe

Ends f.52b. when ȝoure wille is swete lorde god. Amen.

19. f.52b. LOrde fulle of mercy of grace and alle goodnes verrey loue and comfort

Ends f.55. ȝe graunte good lorde and god. Amen.

20. f.55b. O Blysfulle lorde God Jhesu criste delyuerer of soules

Ends f.57b. lede vs þeder þat vs hath made and bouȝte. Amen.

21. f.57b. LOrde god I þat am made werke of youre feyre handes

Ends f.59. and lowyng mote be nowe and euer. Amen.

22. f.59. O lorde þat ben the lawde of my soule

Ends f.60. to worschip ȝowe endelesly. Amen.

23. f.60. O God lorde remembre yowe of youre grete louande mercy

Ends f.61b. And reste in blysse wyth ȝowe. Amen.

24. f.61b. O Blysfulle lorde verrey god þat loued me a fore

Ends f.64. blysfulle worlde þat is to come. Amen.

25. f.64. O ȝe kynge of honoure þat vs hath made so ryche

Ends f.67. worschipe and plesyng to ȝowe. Amen.

26. f.67. LOrde god almyȝty soueraynly wyse and soueraynly benynge

Ends f.68b. of alle creatours nowe and euer. Amen.

27. f.68b. Gloryous god be whome nowe I haue founde
Ends f.71. and to haue nowe and euer. Amen.

28. f.71. Souerayne lorde and kynge euerlastynge god þat euer leuyth and no þing dyeth
Ends f.74b. wyth outen ende euerlastynge god Amen.

29. f.74b. My3tfulle lorde god wyth outen mortalyte
Ends f.79. in blysse wyth outen ende. Amen.

30. f.79. Ryght dere god 3e beth he þat enlumyneth
Ends f.82. it may be so after 3oure grete bountee. Amen.

31. f.82. O 3e my grete desyre lorde god
Ends f.87b. & dwel thurh endeles worlde. Amen.

32. f.87b. The xxxii Chapiter
O Gode lorde 3efe it be plesyng to 3ou
Ends f.92. that I so gretly desire to see. Amen amen so mote it be. Amen for charite.

214. A meditation and prayer for grace. Harley 5036. f.13. s.xv.
19 lines to page.

R. A meditacion and prayer for grace to obserue the perfect tru Religion of Criste.

Beg. O blessid Jhesu equalle god with the fader of heuyn

Ends f.18b. be parteyner of thy joy celestiall Amen.

215. A meditation and prayer for grace. Harl.5036.f.9b. s.xv.
19 lines to page.

R. A meditacioun and prayer for grace to knowe þe lawes of men & to obserue them bothe.

Beg. O blessed lorde god omnipotent whiche art all and in alle thingis

Ends f.12b. for myne offence & synne and to haue mercy vppon me Amen.

216. A Meditation and prayer upon entering church. Harley 5036.f.1. s.xv.
19 lines to page.

R. A meditacioun & prayer whan þou entrest into the Chirche.

Beg. O blessed lorde which of thy bounteous goodnesse hast this day

Ends f.3b. so to be parteyner of thy eternalle glori Amen.

217. A meditation and prayer for grace. Harley 5036.f.7b. s.xv.
19 lines to page.

R. A meditacioun & prayer for grace to haue the true faith wherby we be Justifyed.

Beg. O gracious god which of thy charitable goodnesse doste giffe

Ends f.9. by thy only grace shalt haue Justified. Amen.

218. A meditation and prayer for grace. Harl. 5036.f.19. s.xv.
19 lines to page.

R. A meditacon & prayer onli to god for grace & to none other saint nor creature.

Beg. O lord and fader almyghty wiche of thy greate bounteousnes

Ends f.21. I may be partaker of þe Joy celestiall. Amen.

219. A meditation and prayer for grace to know God. Harl.5036.f.4. s.xv.
19 lines to page.

R. A meditacon & prayer for grace to knowe god.

Beg. O thow eternalle god most highe

Ends f.7. I may haue þe fruicioun of þe in the lyffe eternalle. Amen.

220. A meditation and prayer for grace. Harl.5036.f.21. s.xv.

R. A meditacon & prayer for grace to honour god only & to auoyde all Idolatri.

Beg. O Thow moste blessid and gracious lord omnipotent founder of all grace

Ends, imperf., f.22. wiche he reseuyth of thy goodnes

II. CHRIST.[1]

221. Prayer to Christ at the Mass.
Royal 17 C.XVII.f.98b. s.xv.in.
25 lines.

Beg. Hayle, Jhesu, godys sone in þe forme of brede borne of Mary withowtyn syn

Ends f.98b. ay lastyng blys þu putte me in. amen.

222. Prayer showed to a devout person called Mary Ostrewyk. Harl.494.f.61b. s.xv.
25 lines.

R. Certane prayers schewyd vnto a devote persoun callyd Mary Ostrewyk.

Beg. Fyrst. In remembrance of the wounde In þe ryght hande

Ends f.62. The vth when þe syde was opynede with þe spere And then knelyng say veni sancte spiritus

223. Poem to Christ - attributed to Lydgate. Add.34,360.f.59. s.xv.ex.
6 stanzas of 8 lines, thefirst of 7.

Beg. Jhesu Crist kepe oure lyppes from pollucion
As thow suffredist deth for almankynde

Ends f.59b. Or that the swerd be whet of vengeaunce.

---

1. See also items 201, 214.

224. Another copy, Harley 2251.f.1.

Cf. E.P. Hammond, Anglia.28. (1905), pp.1-28 on the poems by Lydgate, inc. items 223 and 224, in MSS. Add.34,360 and Harl.2251.

225. Prayers to Christ. Royal 17 C.XVII.f.97. s.xv.in.

1. Beg. Jhesu Cryste þat dyed on tre
And sofurred pyne for Adam syn
3 stanzas of 12 lines.

Ends. to gif me syn as I dyd ere [?,partially illegible].

2. Beg. Lord, þi flesche was mekyl adrede
Agan þat þu suld pyned be
11 stanzas of 8 lines.

Ends f.98b. To whylke þu as my saule dere bought.

1. pr. by Carleton Brown, Religious Lyrics of the XVth Century, pp.97-8.

226. Orison to the Name of Christ. Arund.285.f.178. s.xvi. 4 lines.

Beg. R. Ane vthir orisoun to þe name of Jhesu.
Jhesu for thy haly name
And for thy bitter passioun

6 lines of verse and 5 of prose.

Ends. We may do our dewte & homage Ilkane with vthir and for vthir Sueit Jhesu Amen.

Other copies: Bodl. 11914,f.134b; Bodl. 18340, f.81a; Bodl. 18344,f.28b; Bodl. 21628,f.35a; New Coll. Oxf. 310,f.115a.
Cf. Robbins, Mod. Phil. XXXVI, p.337; Robbins, Studies in Philology, XXXVI, p.471, etc.

227. Another copy, Harley 2445,f.136.

228. Another copy, Harley 2851,f.31b.

229. Another copy, Sloane 747,f.46b.

230. Another copy, Add.27,924,f.221.

231. The glorious invocation of our Saviour Jesu. Add.33,381. s.xv.
26 lines to page.

R. The glorious Invocacioun of owre sauyour Jhesu.

Begins f.181. Dominus noster Jhesu humiliauit semetipm [sic] pro nobis vsque ad mortem ante crucis
Jhesu Jhesu Jhesu mercy.
Jhesu haue mercy of me and forgyff me the grete offensis Whyche I haue done in the sy3th of the

Ends f.181b. I beseche the and for thy gloryous name Jhesu þe holy trinite son very god haue mercy vpon me.

232. Prayers to our Saviour. Arund.285.f.107. s.xvi.

A series of fifteen prayers, each about 20 lines, with the prayer 'Jhesu, Jhesu, Jhesu haue marcy on me' between each.

a) Jhesu haue marcy on me and forgif me þe gret offencis

b) Jhesu helpe me to curtinn temptacioun of syn

c) Jhesu strenth me in saule and body

d) Jhesu confort me and gif me grace to haue my maist joy

e) Jhesu mak me constant and stabill in fait

f) Jhesu licht me with gaistlie sueitnes

g) Jhesu grant me grace treuly to luf

h) Jhesu grant me grace treuly to dreid the

i) Jhesu grant me grace to remember persistlie the danger of ded

j) Jhesu accept our penance her

k) Jhesu grant me grace to fle ewill cumpany

l) Jhesu grant us grace and specialie in the tyme of temptacioun.

m) Jhesu gif us grace to prospeir persevrandly

n) Jhesu gif us grace and specialie in tyme of temptacioun to fix our mynde

o) Jhesu gif us grace to ordour our life.

233. Orison to the Name of Christ.
Arund.285.f.176b. s.xvi.
12 stanzas of 4 lines.

R. Ane orisoun to þe Naim of Jhesu Crist.

Beg. Jhesu lord that maid me
And with thy blissit blude hes bocht

Ends f.178. And forgif þame all thair miss Amen.

Numerous other MS. copies, cf. Brown & Robbins, Index of Middle English Verse, no.1727. Pr. by Carleton Brown, Religious Lyrics of the XVth Century, pp.98-100 from Harley Charter 58,C.14; and elsewhere. Cf. Harford, Norfolk and Norwich Archaeological Soc. xvii, 221-44 for a collation of the texts of ten of the MSS. Attributed to Richard de Caistre (d.1420), though, as Brown points out (op.cit., p.313). eight of the twelve stanzas already existed in a 14th-century poem (see No.94, Religious Lyrics of the XIVth Century), which served as a basis for de Caistre's more expanded version.

234. Another copy, Cotton Vespasian A.XXV.f.171.

235. Prayer to Christ. Add.27,948.f.63b. s.xv.
8 lines of prose.

Beg. Jhesu my lord Jhesu my god Jhesu my creature [sic]

Ends f.63b. and so god grammercy Amen.

Inserted in a Latin Book of Hours.

236. The Glorious Invocation of Our Saviour Jhesu. Lansdowne 379.f.64. s.xv.
19 lines to page.

R. The glorious Inuocacion of oure sauyour Jhesu.

Beg. Dominus noster Jhesus Christus humiliauit (&c).

Series of prayers beg. f.66.

1. Jhesu strenghten me in body and saule
2. f.66b. Jhesu comforte me and gyffe me grace
3. f.67. Jhesu make me constant & stable
4. f.68. Jhesu light me with gostly wysdom
5. f.69. Jhesu graunt me grace to drede the
6. f.69b. Jhesu graunte me truly to loue the
7. f.70b. Jhesu graunt me grace to Remembre parfitly
8. f.71b. Jhesu sende me here my purgatory

Ends f.72. The holy trynite one very god haue mercy on me.

With occasional short prayers in Latin interspersed.

237. 15 Meditations on Jesus Christ.
Harl.172.f.5b. s.xv.

Beg. Jhesu that arte euerlastynge swetnes & verray blysse of mannys soule thou passyste alle Joye and erthely desyre

Ends f.10b. suche grace that after this tyme & space that I may see thy blessid face Amen.

238. Poem to Christ. Harl.4012.f.106. s.xv.
12 stanzas of 7 lines.

Beg. Jhesu the sonne of mare mylde
The secunde parsone in trinite

Ends f.108b. Whos number is innumeralle.

239. Two Prayers to Jesus Christ, before Communion. Harl.219.f.153b. s.xv.ex.
7 lines.

1. Beg. Loke vpon vs, o Lorde Jesus Christ
owre gode from thy holy habytacle

Ends and through vs, all the people.

2. Beg. Lorde, I am nott worthy that thow enter under the fylthy Roofe of my sowle 11 lines.

Ends f.153b. be made partakers of the most holy body & bloude.

240. Prayer attributed to Saint Augustine. Harl.2339.f.3. s.xv.
17 lines to page.

R. Seynt austyn þe doctour made þis orisoun þat folowiþ.

Beg. Domine Jhesu criste qui huic mundum etc.
Lord Jhesu crist þat comest fro þe bosum
of þe fadir into þis world

Ends f.5b. wiþ þi holy seyntis in blis wiþouten eende amen.

241. Prayer of St. Bede on the Seven Words spoken by Christ on the Cross.
Lansdowne 379.f.74. s.xv.
19 lines to page.

R. This Oreson that foloweth saynte Bede made vppon the seven wordes that cryst spake hongyng on þe cros.

Beg. Lorde Jhesu cryst that spake vij wordes In the last ende of thy lyffe

Ends f.76. for to dwelle into Withoute ende Amen [sic].

See also item 268. Cf. Wilmart, 'Le grand poème Bonaventurien sur les septes paroles du Christ en Croix', Revue Bénédictine. 47. (1935), pp.235-278, for the origins and earlier versions of this devotion. Cf. also Wilmart, 'Prières médiévales pour l'adoration de la croix', Ephemerides Liturgicae. 46. (1932), pp.22-65.

242. Prayer on the Passion. Harl.2339.f.2. s.xv.
33 lines.

R. Þis orisoun þat folowiþ is in mynde of Jhesu cristis passioun.

Beg. DEus qui voluisti pro redempcione mundi etc. Lord Jhesu crist þat woldist for þe aȝenbiynge of þe world

Ends f.3. to be wiþ þin holy aungels wiþouten eende amen.

243. Fifteen O's. Royal 17 C.XVII.f.95. s.xv.in.
36 lines to page, double-columned.

Beg. Lorde Jhesu, euerlastyng swetnes of þam þat þe lof

Ends f.96b. worcheþ þe wyt alle sayntes endlessly amen pater noster Aue.

Early printed texts include: Caxton's Fifteen O's (1491), S.T.C.20195; Wynkyn de Worde's Primer (c.1494), S.T.C.15875; The XV Oes in Englysshe with other prayers (Robert Copland, 1529), S.T.C.20196; Thys prymer in Englyshe and in Latin... (1538), containing the sequence, described as 'The xv. prayers of saynt brygyde'. Wilmart, Revue Bénédictine. 47, (1935), p.274, states that the prayers in their original form in Paris Bib. Nat. MS.Lat.13285,f.126 are attributed to an anonymous recluse living at the end of the 14th century. For the Latin text, see Royal 17.A.XXVII,f.88b. and elsewhere. See also items 259 and 276.

244. Prayers to Christ. Royal 17 C.XVII.f.97b. s.xv.in.
36 lines to page,
double-columned.

1. Beg. Lord Jhesu, my maker, my gaynebyere, all my lyf, all my ioy

Ends.f.98b. With þe in euerlastyng blis lord Jhesu lord Jhesu Qui cum dominum [&c].

2. Prayer to Christ at the Mass.

Beg. Jhesu lord, þat noȝt only wold offere þi selfe for vs

Ends f.98b. Last lines illegible.

245. Prayers to Christ. Harley 494.f.108. s.xv.
26 lines to page.

1. Beg. Most mercyfulle lorde & savyour Jhesu chryst wyche dydest geve syght

Ends f.108. I maye possesse a place yn the day or lyght that neuer knoweth nyght or darknesse. Amen.

2. Beg.f.108b. Lorde and savyor christ Jhesu whom yt hath plesyde to suffer dethe for the saffgarde

Ends f.109. with fruytyon of the deite. Amen.

3. Beg.f.110. My lorde Jhesu chryste graunte me þe strength of grace

Ends f.110. the spirituall & weddynge garment of my sowle. Amen.

4. Beg.f.110b. All hayle moste benigne Jesu ful of mercye

Ends f.110b. and reignes god worlde withoute ende.

246. Poem - 'Ab inimicis nostris defende nos Christe' - attributed to Lydgate. Add.34,360.f.69. s.xv.ex.
9 stanzas of 7 lines.

R. Ab jnimicis nostris defende nos criste.

Beg. MOst souerayne lorde o blisful criste Jhesu ffrom oure enemyes defende vs of oure foone

Ends f.70b. Hym and his moder his peple and his lande.

Other copies, Bodl. 3896,f.199b; Trinity Camb. 601, f.245a and f.318a.
Pr. by Mahir, Einige religiöse Gedichte John Lydgates, Oberviechtach 1910; MacCracken, E.E.T.S., E.S.cvii, pp.212-6, from the Bodley MS.

247. Another copy, Harley 2251, f.10b.

248. Another copy, Harley 7578,f.19a.

249. Prayers to Christ. Harley 494.f.107. s.xv.
7 lines.

1. R. Cast your selfe downe before oure lord prostrate & say this.

Beg. My synnys a lorde are innumbere aboue the sandes of þe sea

Ends, imperf. & haue don euylle in the sight

2. Beg. Vysit we pray the o lord this place where þat we now are

Ends f.107. euer more throughe our lorde Jhesus christe. Amen.

250. A Prayer for the Seven Times Christ shed His Blood. Harl.1706.f.10b. s.xv.
32 lines.

R. Prayers.

Beg. Now now Jhesu for thy circumsycyon
Wha thou was kut so in flesshe & skyn

Ends f.10b. We may reioyse euer thy presence.

Col. Amen.

Other copies, Bodl. 21896,f.9b; Longleat 30,f.53a. Carleton Brown, Religious Lyrics of the XVth Century, pp.133-6 prints a poem, beg.'Jhesu, that alle this worlde hast wroghte', from a Huntington MS., of which this poem forms the Oracio at conclusion.

251. Prayer to Christ. Add.15,216.f.13. s.xv.
12 lines.

Beg. O Blessid Jesu depnes of endeles mercy
I besuch the for the depenes of þi woundes

Ends f.13. þat thy dredefull dome be passid. Amen.

252. Prayer to Christ. Add.15,216.f.33b. s.xv.
25 lines in all.

Beg. O Blessid Jhesu louable kyng and freynd
in all thyng haue mynde of the sorous

Ends f.35b. & geue me conforte in all my desease. Amen.

253. Prayer to Christ. Harl.5036.f.22. s.xv.
19 lines to page.

Beg. O blessede Jheseu make me to loue þe interly,
O most marcifulle Sauioure.

Ends f.25. and possese it holde it and kepe it only to the. Amen.

254. Prayer to Christ. Add.15,216,f.27b. s.xv.
24 lines.

Beg. O Blessyd Jhesu maker of all the world
þat of a man may not be mesured

Ends f.29b. to kepe me with both loue & drede AMEN.

255. Prayer to Christ. Add.15,216.f.16b. s.xv.
15 lines in all.

Beg. O Blessed Jesu moste mekyst lyon myghtiest king

Ends f.17. when my soule shalbe anguished & my spirite trobled Amen.

256. Prayer to Christ. Add.15,216.f.17. s.xv.
12 lines to page.

Beg. O Blessid Jesu the onely begotyn sonne of almyghty god thi father

Ends f.18. to þe which in this life is an outlawe or pilgryme.

257. Prayer to Christ. Add.15,216.f.18. s.xv.
42 lines in all.

Beg. O Blessid Jesu very & trewe plentuus vyne

Ends f.19b. to prayse the with all sayntes in blys. Amen.

258. Prayer to Christ. Add.15,216.f.35b. s.xv.
7 lines.

Beg. O Blessid Jhesu well of endeles pitte þat
said vpon the tre of the holy crosse

Ends ffor mynde of this bles
Breaks off at foot of f.35b. Conclusion lacking.

259. Fifteen O's - paraphrase
by Lydgate. Harl.2255.f.104. s.xv.
9 stanzas of 8 lines.
[42 stanzas in full text]

Beg. O Blyssid lord, my lord, O Crist Jhesu
Welle and hedspryng of eternal swetnesse

Ends f.110b. The chartir asselyd whan thu heeng
on þe Rood.

Other copies, Bodl. 798,f.1a; Bodl. 11914,f.111b; Jesus Camb. 56,f.65b. Pr. by MacCracken, E.E.T.S., E.S.cvii, pp.238-50 from Bodl. 798.
See also items 243 and 276.

260. Another copy, Add.29,729,f.11 and at f.287a
(begins imperf. at stanza 31).

261. Prayers to Christ for each day
of the week. Harley 494.f.20b. s.xv.
c.15 lines to page.

Beg. Sonday O good Jhesu I beseche the make
me to love the fervently

Ends f.21b. and comytte me hooly vnto the booth
boody & sowle. In manas tuas, etc.

262. Prayer to Christ -
O bone Jhesu. Harl.2339.f.8. s.xv.
17 lines to page.

R. Here folowiþ a precious orisoun for him þat
loueþ þis name Jhesu.

Beg. O Bone Jhesu etc. O good Jhesu. O mekeste
Jhesu. O swettist Jhesu.

Ends f.9b. & alle þat louen þi name Jhesu amen.

Cf. H.E. Allen, Writings ascribed to Richard Rolle, p.314.

263. Expostulatory prayers to Christ. Add.10,596.f.54b. s.xv.
22 lines to page.

Beg. O Good Jhesu o mercifullist Jhesu o pitefulest Jhesu

Ends f.55b. among alle hem þat louen þi swete name Jhesu Amen.

A series of 7 brief prayers.

264. Prayer to Christ. Add.15,216.f.32b. s.xv.
21 lines in all.

Beg. O Jesu blessid mirror of endeles clerenes

Ends f.33b. to shew thy mercy to me in the oure of my deth. Amen.

265. Prayer to Christ. Add.15,216.f.25. s.xv.
62 lines in all.

Beg. O Jesu endles swetenes of louyng sowles

Ends f.27b. trewe confession and satisfaccion & of all my synnes deue remission Amen.

266. Prayer to Christ. Add.15,216.f.29b. s.xv.
29 lines.

Beg. O Jesu heuenly leche haue mynde of thi langor

Ends f.31b. be to me plenary remission & forgeuenes of my synnys.

267. Prayer to Christ. Add.15,216.f.31b. s.xv.
22 lines.

Beg. O Jesu very fredome of angels padise [sic] of all goostely delytes

Ends f.32b. agenste there willys under the wynges of thi blessid passion. Amen.

268. Orison on the Seven Words.
Arund.285.f.163. s.xvi.
10 stanzas of 5, 7 or 8 lines.

R. Heir followis ane deuoit orisoun to be said in the honour of þe seuin wordis that our saluiour spak apoun þe croce.

Begins O Lord God O Jhesu Crist
O sueit saluiour I þe salewe

Ends f.164b. And praise thy fair face Amen.

Pr. by Carleton Brown, Religious Lyrics of the XVth Century, pp.142-4. See also item 241.

269. Prayer to Christ. Add.16,609.f.236b. s.xv.ex.

Beg. O lorde Jhesu Cryste which hathe promysed to oure olde fathers the temporall goode

Ends f.236b. and that in all thinges may perpetually please the.

Follows conclusion of Ludolphus of Saxony's Life of Christ in MS.

270. Prayer to Christ. Harley 494.f.75. s.xv.
c.15 lines to page.

R. heraftir foloweth a deuoute meditacioun and a thankefulle orison to owre lorde for his mannyfold giftes and benefettes

Beg. O my lord & god Jhesu Christ the sonne of the eternalle god

Ends f.82b. in blysse euermore abidynge. Qui vivis & regnat etc. Deo gracias.

271. Poem - 'O Sapiencia qui ex ore'.
('The Seven O's of Christ').
Harley 45.f.168. s.xv.
86 lines in all.

Beg. O sapiencia of þe ffader surmountyng all thyng
Procedyng from his mowth his hestis to fulfill

Ends f.169. In þe ryght wysnesse swet Jhesu þat I be delyuered. Amen.

Col. Iste liber constat domine margarete
Brente cum magno honore Amen.

Pr. by Carleton Brown, Religious Lyrics of the XVth Century, pp.90-2, from this MS.

272. The bedes of St. Gregory's Prayer. Harley 494.f.105. s.xv.
17 lines to page.

R. Here folowis þe bedes of pardon in englyshe of saynt gregorieys pytye.

Beg. O swete blessyde Jhesu for thy holy name
& thy byttere passioun

Ends f.105b. in heven to see thy blessyde face.
Say at euery verse a pater noster & aue
in alle with on credo.

273. Ane dewoit exercitioun. Arund.285.f.94. s.xvi.
22 lines to page.

R. Her followis ane dewoit exercitioun to be said euer ilk sonday in þe honour of þe croun of thorne and pains quhilkis our sawuour Jhesu thollit in his blist heid The Rubrik followis

[Rubric almost identical]

Beg. f.95. O sweet Jesu crist sone of god of life
I synfull and vnworthy creatour

The prayer is divided in seventeen sections, each beginning with a variation on the phrase 'O sueit lord I desir hertlie to thank you' and with the prayer 'Haill maist lovsum lord Jhesu crist' etc., between each section.

Ends f.106b.

274. Prayer to Christ. Harl.2339.f.1. s.xv. 44 lines.

Lacks first leaf.

Beg., imperf., f.1. þere þi modir, make þou þat þi loue & þi charite

Ends f.2. & forto dwelle wiþouten eende amen.

275. Contemplations before Matins, etc. Arund.286.f.129 s.xv. 29 lines to page.

R. Contemplacoun byfore matyns þat þou schalt inwardly þenke & haue in mynde.

Beg. Þou scalt þenke deuoutly & inwardly on þe tyme & on þe place þat oure lord & oure saueour Jhesu crist was borne ine

Ends f.134. fro þee þat lyuest & regnest wiþoute ende lord of euerlastynge ioy & blisse. Amen.

A series of subjects for meditation, rather than actual prayers, before Matins, Prime, Undern, Midday, None, Evensong, Compline, and at Night, with a section on 'What things make a man holy'. Concludes with the prayer

F.134. Lord into þi power & þi kepynge & into þi holy angelis I bytake me body & soule ... 18 lines...[f.134] þat lyuest & regnest wiþoute ende lord of euerlastynge ioy and blisse Amen.

276. Fifteen Oes   Arund.285.f.85   s.xvi.

About 22 lines per page. At head of each opening xv ois on l. and r. page as running title. 'Pater noster' as rubric in red at beginning of each poem, and 'Orate' also at beginning of second.

R. Ois.

a) f.85. To þame þat luffis þe in cheynnis
Thy Joy passis all Joying

Ends f.86. Or I out þis warld pas.

b) f.86. O Jhesu of þe warld maker
And of It als þe gouernour

Ends f.86b. Grant me þe leifand lif lestand.

c) f.86b. O Jhesu hevinlie medicinar
Think on þat langour & þat cair

Ends f.87. Be to me full remissioun.

d) f.87. O Jhesu crist that we on call
Verray fredome of angellis all

Ends f.87b. And ay to wyn with þem fell.

e) f.87b. O Jhesu of Cleynnes þe merroure
Think on þe diseis and dollour

Ends f.88. To wynnyng steid for euermair.

f) f.88. O Jesu Crist king maist aimabill
ffrend and oure all mais ȝairnable

Ends f.88b. Grant me þe Joy þat euer sall lest.

g) f.88b. O Jhesu crist þe well of sweit
Off taist þat euir was perlis ȝit

Ends f.89. That may my saule to blis ay bring.

h) f.89. O Jesu our hertlie sweitnes
Off gude mynd Ichand wytnes

Ends f.89. Sweit saviour I bid grant me þis.

i) f.89. O Jhesu crist riall vertu
Joy of our mynd þat euer is new

Ends f.89b. And all my fremdis mair and myn.

j) f.89b. O Lord Jesu but begynnyng
And almichty Lord but ending

Ends f.90. Grant me þe blis neuer sall haue end.

k) f.90. O Jhesu crist full of marcy
ffor þe deipnis now I þe pray

Ends f.90b. Gracius god here my prayer.

l) f.90b. O Jesu mirrour of clennes
And taikin of all suthfastnes

Ends f.91b. Bruke þe bliss with sanctis feir.

m) f.91b. O Jesu lioun maist strenthy
King vnendlik and ay almytj

Ends f.91b. To lestand blis þat it ma ga.

n) f.91b. O Jesu christ allanerlie
As sone of god almytj

Ends f.92. Me banist pilgrame to þe bryng.

o) f.92. O Jhesu crist verray vyne tre
Haue mynd of þe gret largite

Ends f.93. Thow steid it quhair þi sanctis is.

R. Pater noster, Aue, Credo,
Quhen ȝe haue said yor ois to ane end
Than say þis orisoun till a commend

p) f.93b. Sweit lord I thank þe as I can
That michtlie þi panis begane

Ends f.94b. We mot com quhair all sanctis is.

See also items 243 and 259.

277. Prayers for each day of the week. Lansdowne 379.f.41. s.xv.
19 lines to page.

Beg. Worsship not only of oon [two words illegible] dropes

Ends f.52. to dyuers persones in late dayes by the vartu of the forsaid prayers.

Col. begins f.52. A monke of the Chartre hous of London sent in Wryting the Rule of Reuelacion of the forsaid prayer

Ends f.54. Which copy I wrotte for hym & he caused oþeres to do þe same.

III. THE BLESSED VIRGIN.

278. Poem to the Virgin - attributed to Lydgate. Add. 34.360. f. 60. s. xv. ex.

62 lines; 8-line stanzas, the first and the last of 7.

R. Alle hayle Mary ful of grace
Oure lorde of hevene is with the.

Beg. His mansyoun in the made he has
Also of the borne shal he be

Ends f. 60b. Sith angelis and devils knele thereto.

Pr. by Carleton Brown, Religious Lyrics of the XVth Century, pp. 28-9, from Harley 2251. f. 1b. See also item 282.

279. Another copy, Harley 2251. f. 1b.

280. Prayer to the Virgin. Arund. 318. f. 152. Not dated in cat. 15th C. hand.

R. Oratio et honore percie
ducissa Buckhammie

Beg. Gawde virgine and mother beinge
to criste Jhesu bothe god and kinge

24 lines.

Ends This preir compiled of vertuous memorie
By the Right noble duches buckghammie
Whos soule perdon late elener percie

Catalogue states 'by Eleanor Percy, Duchess of Buckingham'.

281. Aue Maria in English, with note on indulgences. Add. 10,036. s. xv. 24 lines to page.

R. Salutacio beate marie

Beg. f. 92. Aue maria &c. Haile be þou marie ful of grace. oure lord is with þee

Ends f. 92b. and so is þe somme of perdoun mo wyke an hundred
Imperfect.

Cf. H. Thurston, Familiar Prayers, their origin and history, 1953, pp. 90-114 for an account of the origin of this prayer and translations of it. Cf. also Wells, Manual of Writings in Middle English, p. 530. A 14th-century version is in Arund. 57, f. 96b. See also item 278.

282. Prayer to the Blessed Virgin. Add. 39,574. f. 5. s. xv. in. 320 lines, in couplets.

Beg. HAyle, bote of bale, blissed Qwene!
To sight so semely is noon sene

Ends f. 12b. And bryng vs alle to þi sone blys.
Amen.

Pr. by M. Day, E.E.T.S., O.S. 155, pp. 6-15 from this MS.

283. Prayer to the Virgin - Ave gloriosa. Arund. 285. f. 193. s. xvi. 23 irregular stanzas of 4-6 lines.

R. Ane deuoit orisoun To oure Lady The Virgin mary callit Aue Gloriosa.

Beg. HAIll Glaid and glorius
Haill virgin hevinns queyne

Ends f. 197. Thou bair þe lambe of Innocence
Finis.

With coloured woodcut of the Annunciation.

284. Prayer to the Virgin by St. Bernard. Arund. 285. f. 189b. s. xvi.
c. 22 lines to page.

R. Sanct barnald writtis this orisoun of our lady And sayis as gold wes and is maist precius aboue all vthir mettell Sa this orisoun exellis all uther vrisouns And this wes schawin to him be þe Angell.

Beg. Haill mary maist meik sa vesall of the trinite

Ends f. 190. with me with his precius blude Apoun þe cruce Amen.

With coloured woodcut of the Virgin and Child with St. Anne.

285. Prayer to the Virgin - Sancta Maria Mater Dei. Arund. 285. f. 183. s. xvi.
c. 22 lines to page.

R. Ane deuoit orisoun till oure lady callit Sancta maria mater die.

Beg. HAIll Mary the mothur of euermair blist virgin quhilk is comitit

Ends f. 183b. and the haly spreit euerlestand in the bliss of hevin Amen.

With coloured woodcut of saint bearing chalice. See also item 296.

286. Prayer to the Virgin - Ave cuius conceptio. Arund. 285. f. 188b. s. xvi.
c. 22 lines to page.

R. Ane deuoit orisoun till our lady callit aue cuius concepcio.

Beg. HAIll mary quhais concepcioun was cause of our mirthe and consolacioun

Ends f. 189. Pray for us lady euermair to do sa heir we may cum þair Amen.

Second part begins f. 189. R. Oratio.

O Lord god quhilk confortis us and makes us blith

Ends f. 189. þe hour to be blyth with þe in þe joy of hevin Amen.

With coloured woodcut of the Virgin and Child with St. Anne.

287. Salve regina. Add. 37,049. f. 29b. s. xv. in.
40 lines.

R. Salue regina mater misericordie ... [etc., giving Latin text in brief form].

Beg. f. 29b. Hayl oure patron & lady of erthe
Qwhene of heuen and emprys of helle

Ends f. 30. Hayle & fare wele & þinke on me Amen.

In five stanzas. With drawing of Virgin and Child and a figure kneeling at foot. Pr. by Carleton Brown, Religious Lyrics of the XVth Century, pp. 47-48. Cf. also Brunner, Anglia LXI. p. 140

288. Prayer to the Virgin -
Obsecro te. Arund. 285. f. 190. s. xvi.
c. 22 lines to page.

R. Ane orisoun to our lady callit Obsecro.

Beg. I PRay yow lady mary deir
Goddis mothir and madin cleir

Ends f. 193. Well of piete And mercy Amen

With coloured woodcut of the Virgin and Child with St. Anne.

289. Prayers to the Virgin -
Three rose garlands Arund. 285. f. 197. s. xvi.
c. 22 lines to page.

R. Heir begynnis þe thre Roiss Garlandis of the Glorius virgin mary contenand þe Life and Passioun of Jhesu Crist.

The Rubrik. Gif yow desiris to be cleny of syn
And to be riche of verteuis

The prayers are arranged in three sections corresponding to the Mysteries of the Rosary. On f. 198b. an insert coloured woodcut of the Virgin and Child, f. 204b. an insert woodcut of the Pieta, f. 208b. insert woodcut of the Virgin and Child with St. Anne.

Ends f. 213. that bocht me apoun þe croce with his precius blud and dede.

290. Prayer to Our Lady. Add.39.574.f.57b. s.xv.in.
6 lines.

Beg. MArye, Goddis modir dere,
Socoure & helpe us while we ben here

Ends f.58. And helpe us in oure nede.

Pr. by M. Day, E.E.T.S., O.S.155, p.73 from this MS.

291. Prayer to the Virgin and several of the Saints. Arund.249.f.6b. s.xv.
9 stanzas of 7 or 8 lines.

Beg. Mercyful quene as þe best kan and may
after your loue of wreches take pyte

Ends f.7b. To pray for þoure and myn joyfull metyng.

292. Prayers to the Virgin - the Lang Rosair. Arund.285.f.213. s.xvi.
c.22 lines to page.

R. Heir endis þe thre Goldin garlandes of oure lady And begynnis the lang Rosair of þe glorius Virgin mary contenand þe lif and passioun of our Sueit saluiour Jhesu In þe samyn maner & forme þat all man and woman sayand it sawe.

F.213b. Insert coloured woodcut of the Annunciation.

Beg. Mothir of god Quhilk hes consavit and borne our saluiour Jhesu be vertu of þe haly gaist.

Lacuna of one page length, f.220b-221.

Ends f.224. to be to þe with inefabill beatitude and felicite of þe maist exellent and glarius Trinite Amen.

Col. Sic est finis.

293. Prayer to the Virgin. Add.15.216.f.13b. s.xv.
12 lines to page.

Beg. O Blessid myrrour of trewth, taken of vnite

Ends f.15. I mey contenue in prasing and thankyng þe to my lyues end.

294. Prayer to the Virgin. Harl.494.f.87b. s.xv.
19 lines to page.

Beg. O glorious lady quene & empresse of heuen and erthe

Ends f.88b. with the fader sonne and holy gost thre persones and on god. Amen.

295. Prayer to the Virgin - Sancta Maria Mater Dei. Arund.285.f.183b. s.xvi.
c.22 lines to page.

R. Ane devoit orisoun till our lady In inglis callit sancta maria mater dei regina celi et terre.

Beg. O haly mary quene of hevin and erd mothir of our lord Jhesu crist I commend in thy haly and venerabill handis

Ends f.185. and walk in þe my god honoure and glour eternalie Amen.

With woodcut of Virgin and Child. See also item 286.

296. The Seven Sorrows of Our Lady. Harl.494.f.101. s.xv.
c.15 lines to page.

R. Here after folowith the vij sorowes of oure blessid lady.

Beg. O lady Mary temple of the trinite & moder of god

Ends f.104. lady I beseche the.

297. Salutations of the Blessed Virgin. Harl. 494. f. 84b. s. xv. 24 lines.

Beg. O lady most prudent most wyse

Ends f. 85. I salute the with the same etc.

298. Prayer to the Virgin - Ave Maria Alta. Arund. 285. f. 186a. s. xvi. c. 22 lines to page.

R. Ane deuoit orisoun till our lady callit aue maria alta.

Beg. O mary the hie kinrid of the lile of Chaistite

Ends f. 187. Sall all þe frutfull dew of hevin of godlie sueitnes & deuocioun Amen.

299. Prayer to the Virgin - O clementissime! Arund. 285. f. 178b. s. xvi. c. 22 lines to page.

R. The orisoun callit O Clementissime.

Beg. O maist marcifull lady and sweitest virgin Sanct Mary Mother of god maist fulfillit of all piete

Ends f. 181b. maist lowsum virgin mary mothir of god and of marcy Amen.

With 11 lines note on indulgence attached to this prayer, and coloured woodcut of Virgin and Child.

300. Prayer to the Virgin - s. xvi. O Illustrissima et excellentissima. Arund. 285. f. 181b.

R. Heir begynnis ane vthir deuoit orisoun till oure lady callit O Illustrissima et excellentissima.

Beg. O maist nobill and maist excelland glorius and euermair virgin mary mothir of our lord

Ends f. 183. Off him quhome þou bure of þi bosum oure saluioure Jesu christ thy blissit sone Amen.

With woodcut of the Virgin and Child.
c. 22 lines to page.

301. Prayer to Our Lady and St. John. Harl. 494. f. 82b. s. xv.
19 lines to page.

R. A deuoute prayer to oure lady and to seynt Johan the euangelist tawght by our lady to seynt Edmond þe bisshope.

Beg. O intermerata & in eternum benedicta etc. O pure & blessid form euer singlere & incomparable

Ends f. 84b. as he is owre aduocate and comfortare all fulle of benignite. Amen.

See also items 304 and 307.

302. Prayer to the Virgin. Cotton. Titus. C. XIX. f. 120. s. xv.
21 lines to page.

R. This is a deuoute prayer to oure lady.

Beg. O Thou blessed virgine marie cristis modir dere and glorious mediatrixe

Ends f. 121. & lady of the worlde & emperis of helle. Amen.

303. Prayer to the Virgin - O Intemerata. Arund. 285. f. 185. s. xvi.
c. 22 lines to page.

R. Ane deuoit orisoun till our lady callit O Intemerata.

Beg. O Vnfilit and euerlesting blissit singular and incomperabill virgin mary

Ends f. 186b. Quhilk with the father and sone regins eternalie be all warld of warldis Amen.

With woodcut of the Virgin and Child.
Cf. Wilmart, Auteurs spirituels et textes devots, pp. 474-504 on the history of this prayer.
See also items 302 and 307.

304. Prayers taught by the Virgin to St. Bridget. Royal.17 C.XVIII.f.133. s.xv.

Beg. Þe modir of crist tawte seynt brigitte remedieȝ a ȝeennes dyweres temptacyoneȝ

Ends f.133. þat my warkeȝ cume to a good eende Amen.

305. Prayer to the Virgin - Stabit mater dolorosa. Arund.285.f.187. s.xvi. c.22 lines to page.

R. Ane deuoit orisoun till our lady callit stabit mater dolorosa.

Beg. The moder of god stude besyid the croce drery

Ends f.188b. the swerd of dollour persit in the hour of thy passioun be the our lord Jhesu Crist Saluiour of þe warld king of glore Amen.

With woodcut of Our Lady of Sorrows.

306. Prayer to the Virgin - O intemerata. Harl.2339.f.6. s.xv. 17 lines to page.

R. Þis orisoun þat folowiþ schal be seid to oure ladi and to seint Joon þe euangelist.

Beg. O intemerata & in eternum etc. Vnwemmed & wiþouten ende blessid aloone maide wiþoute peer.

Ends f.7b. god wiþouten eende. Amen.

See also items 302 and 304.

307. Prayer to the Virgin, to grant sleep. Harl.541.f.228b. s.xv. 7 lines of verse

B. Vpon my Ryght syde y ma leye bleside lady to the y pray

Ends f.228b. Bleside be the blossomm that sprang lady of the
In nomine patris & filij & spiritus sancti amenn.

Pr. by Carleton Brown, Religious Lyrics of the XVth Century, p.194, from this MS.

308. Prayer to the Virgin for grace. Add. 31.042.f.80. s.xv. 22 stanzas of 8 lines.

Beg. With humble hert I praye iche creature
lorde & lady knyghtes & otheres fferalle

Ends f.81b. O fflorum flos O fflos
pulcherimme

Col. Explicit Cantus Amen.

Cf. MacCracken, Archiv, CXXXI, pp.60-3. This copy lacks first stanza.

309. Another copy, Harley 3869,f.366b.

Beg. Myght wisdom goodnesse of the Trinite
(in 23 stanzas).

IV. SAINTS

310. Invocation to Saint Anne - Lydgate. Add.16.165.f.247. s.xv.med.
11 stanzas of 8 lines.

R. Invocacioun by Lidegate to Seynte Anne.

Beg. Þou first moeuer þat causest euery thing
To haue his keping & thoroughe prouydence

Ends f.248. Sich he be bought with his blood so deer.

Another copy, Bodl.6943,f.44b. Pr. by MacCracken, E.E.T.S., E.S.cvii, pp.130-3, from this MS.

311. Prayer to Saint Barbara. Add.15.216.f.61b. s.xv.
20 lines.

R. A praier to saynte barbara.

Beg. Blessid virgyn of god seynt barbara

Ends f.62b. to be mediatrice for vs to the glorious trinite. Amen.

312. Confession and Prayer of St. Brendan. Harl.1706.f.84. s.xv.
34 lines to page, double-columned.

R. Here begynneth a confessyon whyche ys also a prayere þat Seynt Brandon made and hit ys ryghte nedeffulle to a Chrysten man to sey, and to wyrche þerafter.

Beg. I knowlege me to the thow hyghe increate
And euerlastyng trynyte

Ends f.85. Wherfor I crye the lorde Jhesu cryste mercy. Amen.

313. <u>Prayer to St. Edmund -</u>
<u>Lydgate.</u> <u>Harl. 2255</u>. f. 152. s. xv.
9 stanzas of 8 lines.
(wanting st. 1-3.)

Beg. [stanza 4].
Our helpe our sucour our mediatour most cheefe
As thou arte kyng and prince of this cuntre

Ends f. 153. Callyng to the for helpe in ther moost nede.

Col. Explicit quod lydgate.

Other copies, <u>Bodl. 798</u>. f. 19a; Camb. Univ. Kk. 1. 6. f. 202a. Pr. by MacCracken, <u>E. E. T. S.</u>, E. S. cvii, pp. 124-7 from the Bodley MS.

314. <u>Prayer to St. George.</u> <u>Add. 15. 216</u>. f. 58. s. xv.
29 lines.

R. A prayer to seynte George.

Beg. O Blessyd martyr of god saynt george to the be gyuen lawde and glorie

Ends f. 59. be one of the nombre of the chosen people of heuen Amen.

315. <u>Prayer to St. John.</u> <u>Add. 39. 574</u>. f. 58. s. xv. in.
6 lines.

Beg. SEynt Iohn, for grace þou craue
Þat of his mercy he wole us saue

Ends f. 58. In heuene blis wiþ hym to rest. Amen.

Pr. by M. Day, <u>E. E. T. S.</u>, O. S. 155, p. 73 from this MS.

316. <u>Hymn to St. John the</u>
<u>Baptist.</u> <u>Add. 39. 574</u>. f. 12b. s. xv. in.
10 stanzas of 14 lines.

Beg. BLissed be thow, Baptist, borne & forth broght
Of a byrde baran, bales to bete

Ends f. 15b. Þat heuen be oure mede.

Pr. by M. Day, <u>E. E. T. S.</u>, O. S. 155, pp. 15-19, from this MS.

317. Prayer to St. John the Baptist. Add.15.216.f.59. s.xv. 22 lines.

R. A Prayer to saynte John baptyste.

Beg. Moste blessid and holy precursor of oure lorde

Ends f.60. be mediator for me to the trinite by thie holly intercessiones.

318. Prayer to St. Katherine. Arund.168.f.65b. s.xv. 15 lines.

Beg. Kateryne of kynges blode virgyne & noble martur

Ends f.65b. the first frutes of þi holy bataile.

319. Prayer to Saint Katherine. Add.15.216.f.60. s.xv. 26 lines.

R. A Prayer to saynt katheryne.

Beg. O Swet spouse of oure sauiour blessyd virgen and martir saynt katheryn

Ends f.61. to thie gloriouse spouse criste Jhesu at the oure of my dethe Amen.

320. Prayer to St. Leonard. - Lydgate. Harl.2255.f.114. s.xv. 6 stanzas of 8 lines, the last of 6.

Beg. REste and Refuge to folk disconsolate ffadir of pite and consolacioun

Ends f.115. Wher aungelis ar wont to syngen Osanna.

Col. Explicit.

Other copies, Bodl. 798,f.21a; Jesus Camb. 56,f.75b; Sidney Suss. Camb. 37,f.142b. Pr. by MacCracken, E.E.T.S., E.S.cvii, pp.135-6 from Bodley MS, and by Halliwell, Percy Soc. II, pp.205-6 from this MS.

321. Prayer to St. Mary Magdalene.
Harl. 667. f. 100b. s. xv.
10 lines.

Beg. Seint marie magdalene lady ffay and brithȝ

Ends f. 100b. I besek kithe þat on me & on my ffrendes ilkone.

On a blank leaf in a collection of legal documents.

322. Three Prayers to St. Robert of Knaresborough.
Egerton 3,143. s. xv. ex.
About 25 lines to page.

1. R. Oracio Presidentis.
Beg. f. 35b. Hayle! Saint Robert, a confessoure

Ends f. 37b. Amen, Amen per charite.

In 47 couplets.

2. R. Oracio ad beatum Robertum.

Beg. f. 37b. Hayle! heremete mast þat ys of myght

Ends. f. 38b. I beseke the grauntte me this. Amen.

In 29 couplets.

3. R. A prayer.

Beg. f. 63. Hayle! cheftane, Christes aghen confessour

Ends f. 63b. Ryghtwys Roberd, pray for þis! Amen.

In 18 couplets.

Pr. by Bazire, E.E.T.S., O.S. 228, pp. 76-81, from this MS.

V. THE HEAVENLY HOST.

323. Prayers to All Angels. Add.10,596.f.61b. s.xv.
22 lines to page.

1. R. to alle aungeles

   Beg. I Biseche ȝu lowli hertili & deuoutly alle holi aungels

   Ends f.62b. into worldis of worldis amen.

2. R. to all aungeles

   Beg. I Biseche ȝou o holi mychael holi gabriel holi raphael

   Ends f.63b. þat is aboue alle þingis blessid & blissful god in worldis amen.

   Cf. Wilmart, Auteurs spirituels et textes devots, pp.578-582 on prayers to the Holy Angels.

324. Prayer to St. Gabriel. Add.10,596.f.58. s.xv.
22 lines to page.

R. an orisoun to gabriel

Beg. I preie þe noble prince holy gabriel, strengist chaumpioun

Ends f.58b. & in pees bi Jhesu crist oure lord amen.

325. Prayer to St. Michael the Archangel. Add.10,596.f.57. s.xv.
22 lines to page.

Beg. O myȝhel archaungel of god & messanger in priuytees of the hiȝe king

Ends f.58. & regneþ þoruȝ alle worldis of worldis Amen.

326. Prayer to St. Michael the Archangel. Add.10,596.f.55b. s.xv.
22 lines to page.

Beg. Oh oh [sic] seint Myȝhel archaungil of god prince of heuenli knyȝthode

Ends f.57. bi alle worldis of worldis Amen.

327. Prayer to St. Raphael the Archangel. Add.10,596.f.58b. s.xv.
12 lines.

R. An orisoun to raphael archaungil.

Beg. O Thou greet & hiȝ prince holi raphael medicyn of god

Ends f.58b. þat into it flowe euerlasting helpe amen.

328. Prayers to a Guardian Angel. Add.10,596.f.60. s.xv.
22 lines to page.

1. R. an oþer praier.

Beg. Oh aungel to whom y am commyttid & bitaken of god

Ends f.61. we mowe be glad euerlastingli wiþouten eende amen.

2. Beg. HEil & ioie þu swettist spirit

Ends f.61b. & bringe aȝen to me grace of reconsiliacoun of pees & of helpe amen.

Cf. Wilmart, Auteurs spirituels et textes devots, pp.537-558 on prayers to a Guardian Angel.

329. Prayers to a Guardian Angel. Add.10,596.f.59. s.xv.
22 lines to page.

1. R. Her sueþ dyuers praiers to a mannys owne propir aungel.

Beg. O Blisful & blessid aungel of god to whos keping

Ends f.59b. þoruȝ alle worldis of worldis Amen.

2. Beg. f.59b. Oh aungil of god mynystre of heuenes empire

Ends f.60. which is blessid in worldis of worldis amen.

330. Prayer to a Guardian Angel. Cotton. Faustina D,IV.f.76. s.xv.
19 lines.

R. To thy proper Angelle a devowt prayer.

Beg. O Gloryous angelle to whome our blessyd lord

Ends f.79b. I may leue & prayse owre savyour amen.

Imperfect, leaves 76b and 77 being left blank and the central portion of the prayer missing.

331. Prayers to all Apostles and Evangelists. Add.10,596.f.63b. s.xv.
22 lines to page.

1. R. to alle apostlis & euaungelistis.

Beg. We besechen ȝou & wiþ al þe entent

Ends f.64b. þoruȝ worldis wiþouten eende amen.

2. Beg. I praie & biseche ȝou alle apostlis & euangelistis

Ends f.65b. to dwelle in the wie euerlastingli with ȝou amen.

332. Prayer to All Saints. Add.10,596.f.73. s.xv.
22 lines to page.

R. A praier to alle seintis.

Beg. O ȝe alle seintis & chosen of god

Ends f.77. which lyuest & regnest euerlasting god wiþoute eende amen.

333. Prayer to Confessors. Add.10,596.f.69. s.xv.
22 lines to page.

R. Of confessouris.

Beg. O ȝee alle holi confessouris of god

Ends f.70b. þe gloriose maieste of god wiþ hiȝest loue þerto folewing amen.

334. Prayer to the Holy Innocents. Add.10,596.f.67. s.xv.
22 lines to page.

R. Of innocentis.

Beg. O ȝe holi innocentis which bitwixe ȝoure modris brestis

Ends f.67b. deserue of oure lord þe hundrid crowne with ȝou amen.

335. Prayer to Holy Patriarchs.
Add.10,596.f.65b. s.xv.
22 lines to page.

R. A praier to holi patriarkis.

Beg. O ȝe alle holi patriarkis

Ends f.67. þoruȝ worldis of worldis amen.

336. Prayer to Maidens. Add.10,596.f.72. s.xv.
22 lines to page.

R. Of maidens.

Beg. O ȝe holiest & blessidist maidens of crist

Ends f.73. þoruȝ worldis of worldis amen.

337. Prayer to Martyrs. Add.10,596.f.67b. s.xv.
22 lines to page.

R. Of martris.

Beg. O ȝee alle martris of god whiche bi dyuerse kindis

Ends f.69. to gidere wiþ aungels wiþoute eende in heuenes amen.

338. Prayer to Virgins. Add.10,596.f.70b. s.xv.
22 lines to page

R. Of virgins.

Beg. MErci grace & pite we sechen & asken

Ends f.72. bi alle worldis of worldis Amen.

VI. VARIOUS.

(Blessed Sacrament, Confiteor).

339. Prayer to the Blessed Sacrament. Harl.4011.f.2b. s.xv. 40 lines.

R. A devovte Orysoun to þe holy sacrament.

Beg. Heyle holiest body of oure lorde Jhesu Criste þat art now sothfast conteyned

Ends f.2b. by vertewe & grace of þi life blessid without endyng Amen.

Col. Jhesu lord þi blessid liff help & conford oure wrecchid life Amen.

On the origins of prayers at Communion, etc., cf. Wilmart, Auteurs Spirituels et Textes Devots, pp.21-5.

340. Prayer to the Sacrament. Arund.197.f.46b. s.xv.

R. To the Sacramente.

Beg. Hayle holi bodi of owre lorde Jhesu criste þat art now sothfastly conteynid

Ends f.48. with þe in life euerlastinge y beseche þi mercy. Amen.

*341. Prayer at the Elevation.
Add.39,574.f.88. s.xv.in.
21 lines.

R. Here begynneþ a deuoute prayer and an excellent, that schulde distynctly ben seyd and with greet deuocyoun betwene þe Leuacioun of þe Blessid Sacrament and the thridde Agnus Dei.

Beg. HEyl, Jhesu Crist, Word of þe Fadir, Sone of þe Virgyn

Ends f.88b. borun of the Virgyne Modir, haue mercy of us. Amen.

Pr. by M. Day, E.E.T.S., O.S.155, p.100, from this MS. A translation of a Latin Eucharistic Rhythm given by Daniel, Thesaurus Hymnologicus, II,32 and Levis, Anecdota Sacra, p.107, from a missal in the monastery at Novalesa.

342. Prayer to Christ in the Blessed Sacrament. Harl.494.f.1. s.xv.
14 lines

Beg. I do salute the moote [sic] holy body of owre lord

Ends f.1b. in body and in sowle O very Jhesu lorde.

343. Tract on Confession. Sloane 774.f.1. s.xv.
27 lines to page.

R. A forme of a generall confessioun how a man may shewe clerely by þe spices of þe vij deedly synnes all oþer synnes and how euery deedly synne in þis forme is d.. dede in thes perties þoght speche and dede.

Prologue

Beg. Every bodye þat shall be confessede be he neuere soo hye degree

Ends f.2b. Thys forme of confessioun ȝyf it plese ȝowe ȝe mowe by gynne as I wyl wryte.

Form of confession

R. Here begynnyth the confessyon.

Beg. Benedicte etc. I knowleche to almygchty god and to hys blyssid modur marie

Ends f.36b. and penaunce for my synne in the name of holy chyrche. Confiteor deo

Tract on Meditation f.36b.

R. A fforme of meditacyon to styre a man to deuocioun.

Beg. Manye men ther be y hope in relygioun wommen also

Ends f.40. grawnt vs that gracyowsly Jhesu that art almychty now and euere thy mercy. Amen.

Form of Confession II. f.40.

R. A compendyos general confessioun.

Beg. Benedycyte etc. I knowleche to almyhty god and to hys modur

Ends f.45b. Also I haue not louyd myn nehebore ...

Imperf. Remaining leaves contain notes of anniversaries and medical receipts in a later hand.

344. Form of Confession. Harl.1706.f.87. s.xv.
46 lines to page, double-columned.

R. Septem opera misericordie corporalia.

Beg. FEde the hungry yeue drynke to the thrysty

Ends f.87b. lowly wt herte and mouthe crye the mercy. Amen.

Cf. H. Thurston, Familiar Prayers, pp.73-89 on the origins and early versions of the Form of Confession. Cf. also Wells, Manual of Writings in Middle English, item 32, p.360.

345. Form of Confession.
Royal 18 A.X.f.60b. s.xv.in.
30 lines to page.

R. Seynt Edmunde þe archebishope prechid þis confessyon to þe peple to teche hem þe bettere to kunne schryue hem and he hymself seyde it eche day to god.

Beg. God fadir almyȝti þat art oo god in þre persones

Ends þat y mowe come into þe liife wiþoute ende. Amen.
And sey þi confiteor to þe preest whan he goþ to masse.

Pr. from this MS. by Wilfrid Wallace, Life of St. Edmund of Canterbury, 1893, p.362.

346. Form of Confession. Harl.172.f.11. s.xv.
29 lines to page.

Beg. [C]Onfiteor deo celi et beate marie beato benedicto et omnibus sanctis eius et vobis. [I] knowleche me gilty vnto god and to oure lady

Ends f.17b. ffor the whiche I beseche almyghty god of hys endeles mercy and forgifnes ther of.

347. Form of confession. Add.37,075.f.39b. s.xv.ex.
26 lines to page.

Beg. I knowlege me to god & to owre lady

Ends f.40b. & to you my gostly fadyr.

348. Form of Confession. Harl.494.f.91. s.xv.
19 lines to page.

R. Here foloweth a shorte confessionalle for religious persons of euery dayes synnes aftir Bonaventure.

Beg. Confiteor deo beate marie omnibus sanctis et vobis. I knowleg to almighti god to oure blessid lady

Ends, imperf., f.96. and that in specyalle I eny wise

349. Form of Confession. Harl.1706.f.86b. s.xv.
46 lines to page, double-columned.

R. Quinque sensus.

Beg. O thow hyghe excellent lord gode lowly to the I knowleche

Ends f.87. And the blyssede ensaumple yeuyng of the my lorde Jhesu cryste. Amen.

350. Form of confession drawn on the Ten Commandments. Harl.1706.f.85. s.xv.
46 lines to page, double-columned.

R. The x Commaundementys.

Beg. O thow hyghe in comprehensyble increate and euerlastynge trinite

Ends f.86b. thou lyuest and regnest lorde kynge god and man into worldes off worldes. Amen.

351. Form of Confession. Harl.1706.f.87b. s.xv.
46 lines to page, double-columned.

R. Septem opera misericordie spiritualia.

Beg. TEche counseylle Chastyse or repreue comforte

Ends f.88. And thou lorde to whoum strecceth alle the trespasses mercy lorde gode mercy. Amen. Amen.

352. Form of confession.
Royal 18 A.X.f.55b. s.xv.in.
30 lines to page.

R. Modus confitendi in Anglicis verbis.

Beg. Whan þou þenkest to purge þi soule of synne by confessioun

Ends f.60b. y biseche ȝow to pray for me.

353. Prayer in tribulation.
Royal 17.C.XVIII.f.132b. s.xv.
53 lines.

R. A specyall prayer iff þow be in any Angny or greet tribulacyoun.

Beg. Iff þow be in any greet tribulacyoun or aduersite, go in to þe chirche

Ends f.133. & alle my membereȝ þat my warkes cume to a good eende Amen.

LIST OF AUTHORS

INDEX OF MANUSCRIPTS.

Egerton	615.	188, 190, 192.
	2,006.	128.
	2,658.	18.
	3,143.	322.
Harley.	45.	271.
	116.	208.
	172.	117, 237, 346.
	218.	122.
	219.	239.
	372.	72.
	494.	103, 118, 156, 168, 203, 212, 222, 245, 249, 261, 270, 272, 294, 296, 297, 301, 342, 348.
	535.	109.
	541.	307.
	629.	77.
	665.	25.
	667.	321.
	1,304.	78.
	1,671.	155.
	1,704.	30.
	1,706.	9, 39, 141, 151, 157, 161, 250, 312, 344, 349, 350, 351.
	2,251.	24, 29, 64, 65, 70, 74, 91, 96, 98, 101, 108, 123, 247, 279.
	2,255.	2, 4, 5, 7, 56, 66, 90, 99, 102, 104, 120, 178, 209, 259, 313, 320.
	2,339.	94, 153, 196, 205, 240, 242, 262, 274, 306.
	2,382.	22, 79, 124.
	2,445.	227.
	2,851.	228.
	3,810. (Part I)	26.
	3,862.	80.
	3,869.	309.

INDEX OF INITIA.